The Gathas
the Sublime Book of Zarathustra

Khosro Khazai, Ph.D

Copyright © 2007, by Khosro Khazai
All rights reserved

First published by:

European Centre for Zoroastrian Studies
7 Galerie de la Reine, 1000 Brussels-Belgium
Tel. & Fax +32 – 2 / 374.92.60
Email: info@gatha.org
WebSite : www.gatha.org

Translation from Persian to English:
Dr. Parviz Koupai,
14 songs (from song 4 to 17);

Review and correction:
Havovi Patel -Panek

Final review and correction:
Sheila Sylvester

Technical advice and layout:
Azad Aghvami

Cover:
painted by Sam
Flying" Farvahar"
Inspired from the images of "Farvahar"
in Persepolis, flying towards the light

Printed in Nivelles, Belgium

Acknowledgments

The translation of such a complex, profound and poetic book as the one you have in your hands needs the assistance of many people in many different ways.

The English translation from Persian could not be carried out, in such a short time, without the great help of **Dr.Parviz Koupai,** the vice president of *"Zoroastrian Assembly"* in *Anaheim, California,* who translated, 14 songs (from song 4 to 17), and **Dr. Khosro Mehrfar** who acted as coordinator. I am very grateful to them.

My great thanks also go to **Havovi Patel-Panek,** who reviewed with patience the English text and made the necessary corrections.

Particularly, I owe many thanks to **Sheila Sylvester** who put the final touch in re-viewing and largely improving the English text; she has done an excellent work. Also, I must thank **Nadine de Wasseige** who coordinated this task.

I wish to express my deep gratitude to my long time collaborators and friends, **Azad Aghvami,** who took care of the lay-out and solved many technical problems throughout this work, and **Sam** who so artistically designed the cover.

Finally, but by no means least, I must thank **Kerstin Windahl** who has been always my enduring supporter throughout my life.

Khosro Khazai *(Pardis)*

About the author

Doctor Khosro Khazai (Pardis), received his PhD in 1978 from the Universities of Brussels and Ghent in Belgium. He is a specialist in Middle Eastern and Central Asian Studies, focussing principally on the history of Persian civilization, archaeology, linguistics and ideas.
For the past 30 years, he has been a scientific researcher and teacher, in Middle Eastern, Central Asian and Zoroastrian Studies
Dr. Khazai has published nine books, and more than 160 articles. His main books are:
-*Birth and Evolution of Writing* ; *5000 Years of the history of writing*, *(in French), translated also in Dutch, Brussels 1985*
-*From Sumer to Babylonia* ; *(in French), translated also to Dutch, Brussels 1983,*
-*The Book of Existence; a trip into the Zoroastrian existential philosophy* *(in Persian) Paris 1990.*
-*The Wayfarers of Arta; An Experience in the Depths of Zarathustra's Existential Philosophy); (in French); Brussels, 1993.*
-*The Gathas, the Sublime Book of Zarathustra,*
(in Persian) Brussels, 2006
The English version was released in March 2007. The French and Spanish translations will be released at the end of 2007.

Publisher's note

This book appeared first in July 2006 in the Persian language. Immediately after its release and we should say surprisingly, it met such a success that over-passed all our expectations. Not only the subject was an academic matter, both in terms of history of ideas, philosophies and religions, but also it was almost completely unknown to the general public.

As a matter of fact, the Gathas of Zarathustra, widely regarded as a monument of the universal culture, had been considered, for a long time, as a monopoly of the departments of linguistics, philosophy or religions.

it was one of the first times that it had been translated from the near to 4000 years old original Zarathustra's language to a clear, fluid and poetic modern language.

Therefore we decided to translate it from Persian into other languages such as English, French and Spanish.

We are happy that five months after the Persian publication, you have today in your hands, the English translation of this invaluable book.

We do hope you will enjoy reading this new version of *the Gathas, the sublime book of Zarathustra* that took its author *Dr. Khosro Khazai* over five years to accomplish.

Dedicated to
Mobed Mehraban Zartoshty
and Mr.Manoucher Farhangi
the great benefactors

Contents

I-Introduction:

	Pages
About this new version of the Gathas	10
Keys to a better understanding of the Gathas	14
The Aim of Life in the Gathas	19
The Physical and Mental Worlds in the Gathas,	21
Zarathustra's doctrine in the Gathas	22
The attributes of Ahura Mazda and how they Function	26
The Assembly of Magi	31
The Way Zarathustra was teaching	33
The three basic prayers in Zarathustra's doctrine	35
Zarathustra and his family	37
Zarathustra and Europe 2500 years of history	39
Quick reference	47

II-Songs   Pages

Song 1 *(Hat 28)*;   *50*
Zarathustra's prayer for happiness
and power to make the Earth a happy planet

Song 2 *(Hat 29)*;   *55*
Zarathustra is chosen to make
the oppressed Earth a happy planet

Song 3 *(Hat 30)*;   *60*
Good and Evil
and Freedom of Choice

Song 4 *(Hat 31)*;   *66*
Freedom of choice

Song 5 *(Hat 32)*;   *76*
Deceitful Teacher
and False Teachings

Song 6 *(Hat 33)*;   *83*
O Ahura Mazda,
reveal yourself to me

Song 7 *(Hat 34)*;   *90*
Where the light of Ahura Mazda shines,
wisdom shall also appear

Song 8 *(Hat 43)*;   *98*
Happiness is for the one
who makes others happy

Song 9 *(Hat 44)* ;   *107*
Respond to my questions
and tell me why and how

Song 10 *(Hat 45);* **118**
*The two ways of
thinking and living*

Song 11 *(Hat 46)* **124**
*Discouragement,
perseverance and victory*

Song 12 *(Hat 47)* **133**
*Ahura Mazda, the power
that creates and progress*

Song 13 *(Hat 48);* **136**
*The best refuge is an Earth
that Serenity rules over it.*

Song 14 *(Hat 49);* **142**
*Resistance against
oppressive rulers*

Song 15 *(Hat 50);* **147**
*With thought provoking Gathas
I praise You O Mazda*

Song 16 *(Hat 51);* **152**
*Those who are united in
Good Thought, Word and Deed*

Song 17 *(Hat 53);* **162**
*Consult your wisdom,
then choose*

Main sources **167**

*May we be among those who
make this world new and fresh!*
Gathas, song 3, stanza 9

About this new version of the Gathas

Zarathustra announced about 4000 years ago, the core of his doctrine or existential philosophy, in form of 17 songs called the Gathas.
We know that at this time there was no adequate method of transcribing his words, nor any other means of recording them. It is quite extraordinary that after such a passage of time his words now reach us in their original unaltered purity of thought.
Added to this fact, the language in which Zarathustra had proclaimed his doctrine, the Gathas, fell into total oblivion for about 2000 years, to the extent that during this very long period not a phrase could be understood. Yet strangely, not a single word has been missed or added or displaced!
We have to admit that this is a rare phenomenon in the history of ideas and civilisations. The Zoroastrian priests, called *"mobed"*, learned the Gathas by heart and passed them down as an oral tradition from one generation to the next.
Learning them by heart was relatively easy as they were in the form of songs with meters and poetic rhythm.

In the third century, they created an extremely sophisticated alphabetic system of writing able to capture and fix all the nuances, accents and pronunciation of this long forgotten language.
Even though the Gathas could not yet be understood, the alphabet could however be vocalized phonetically as sacred songs in the fire temples.

1500 years later, in the 18th century, the French linguist Anquetil du Perron, who was working among the Zoroastrians of India, (called the *"Parsis"*), made an extremely important discovery. He noticed that the language of the oldest part of the Zoroastrian literature collected together in a book called "the Avesta" looked strangely similar to Sanskrit, the sacred language of India. This was the language in which the Indian religious book *Rig Veda* had been written, and which had been recently discovered. It seemed to offer the key to deciphering the old part of *the Avesta,* namely the Gathas.

Eventually, with hugely painstaking efforts the language of the Gathas was deciphered, even though the content appeared to be very difficult for an accurate translation.
Inevitably many errors and mistakes crept into the translations.
During the past 200 years however, a great number of linguists and researchers from different countries have been working hard on the Gathas texts and every single word of this sublime book has been the subject of passionate debates and innumerable papers, and books have been written on them.

Despite these efforts, a number of errors and misinterpretations have still persisted. These errors were mainly due to a lack of spiritual sensitivity of many translators, all excellent, but too sure of their linguistic knowledge and too preoccupied with word-by-word translation.

This couldn't work. Even though the language in the Gathas is Indo-European, but it is much older, even than Sanskrit. Many thousands of years separate it from modern Indo-European languages.

They are often composed of words whose meaning (though uncertain) can only be determined by the understanding of its spiritual context and the wisdom of its message.

The phrases can often be understood when only the "intention" of the phrase can be approached, touched and captured. That is why the literal translations are often incomprehensible.

This also explains why different translations of the Gathas can differ so much from one another.

Therefore this is why my first aim in carrying out this new research and translation (which is based on my 30 years of academic experience in this field) is to bring more coherence and precision to the key words and to find their exact place in the context. In fact a good understanding of these key words, written in this book in bold, are essential to fully apprehend Zarathoustra's sacred message.

My second aim, a direct consequence of the first one, is to render this new version of the Gathas as close as possible to Zarathustra's thought.

And finally, the last but not the least objective that I have pursued all through this book has been to give more freshness to the texts, avoiding old fashioned words or the words foreign to Zarathustra's doctrine, in order to render his message purer, poetic and more accessible to a greater public.

To carry out this work, I have taken full advantage of the works of those who have spent their whole lives during the past two hundred years until to now in pursuit of a better understanding of the Gathas.
Here, I would like to offer to them all, alive or dead, my highest praise and deepest gratitude.
A list of them is given at the end of this book.
May the names of all those who, in many countries around the world, have tried, or are trying, to make known this sublime doctrine be recorded in history and engraved in our hearts for ever.

Khosro Khazai (Pardis)

Keys to a better understanding of the Gathas

The word "Gathas", in the Old Persian language means "songs" and refers exclusively to the 17 sublime and thought-provoking songs of Zarathustra; they unquestionably belong to the most precious treasures of the world's culture.

Every word of this invaluable book has come from the mouth of Zarathustra dating from almost 4000 years ago. Despite their journey of ages through the countless vicissitudes of history, they have come to us unaltered, with the same original freshness and yet a surprising modernity.

The language, in which the Gathas are composed, is one of the idioms of the Aryan group of Iranian languages. This idiom was spoken about 4000 years ago somewhere in the East of the Iranian highlands, a region situated today in the North East of Iran, West of Afghanistan and South of Tajikistan.

The Gathas' language is related to Sanskrit, the sacred language of India in which the Rig Veda has been written. But the Gathas' grammatical structure and words show that they are older by several centuries than Sanskrit.

We know, since the 19th century, and with the development of "comparative studies of languages", that the language of the Gathas is not only the source of all Iranian languages such as Persian, it is also one of the sources of many European languages.

The Gathas have been composed and arranged in five different meters or poetic rhythms.

These meters follow the Indo-Iranian form of poetry recitation that uses long and short vowels. The whole 17 songs of the Gathas which contain 238 stanzas of around 6000 words, convey the core and essence of Zarathustra's doctrine.

In the Persian Empire, from the 6th to the 3rd century BC. the Gathas, within the Zoroastrian doctrine, were the existential philosophy of this first and huge universal empire that ruled over 28 countries, including Greece, Egypt, India, and whole of the Middle and Near East countries.
However with the collapse of the Persian Empire in the 3rd Century BC. and the destruction, burning and looting of Persepolis, Susa, and their libraries by the armies of Alexander of Macedonia, and the consequent disintegration of that brilliant civilisation that had given to the world the first "Charter of Human Rights" (now in the British Museum), - a dreadful catastrophe with regard to the Gathas occurred. The language of the Gathas spoken only in a small region of that Empire, slowly faded away and eventually was forgotten. This oblivion was going to last over 2000 years.

Very soon, another Persian dynasty from the North of Iran, (the Parthians) chasing the Greeks, imposed its rule not only over Iran, but also over the whole of Central Asia, and the Middle and Near East.
Their very long rule was going to last almost 500 years from 248 BC. to 224 AC.

In order to restore, once again, the Zoroastrian identity of Iran and the Central Asian countries, they started to search for and assemble the remaining Zoroastrian texts that were scattered far and wide.
They gathered these scattered texts, and arranging them in a collective book and named it "The Avesta", meaning *"inner knowledge"*. It is said that The Avesta in its complete form was made up of 21 books; today only one third of it has reached us.

However none of the Avestan texts, except the Gathas, were composed by Zarathustra. They were all written by persons of whom we know nothing, neither their names nor their functions.
Many of these texts were written either hundreds or even more than one thousand years after Zarathustra, or they belonged to pre-Zoroastrian religions (the very religions that had been rejected and fought against by Zarathustra himself).

During the period of oblivion into which the language of the Gathas had fallen, many tried to guess what Zarathustra had said. Every one offered his or her own interpretations, views and opinions. Meaningless rituals and myths, both pre-Zoroastrian and post-Zoroastrian, were introduced, and beliefs completely foreign to the original sublime doctrine of Zarathustra (which was based entirely on reason and wisdom, as expressed in the Gathas), entered into "The Avesta" in the name of Zarathustra.
Out of Zarathustra's supposed sayings or the interaction with the newly born religions such as the Christianity, other religions such as Manichaeism appeared in the 3rd century

and the first communist doctrine called Mazdekism after the name of its founder Mazdak emerged in the 5th century.
The forgotten language of 'The Gathas' caused the distortion of Zoroastrianism far from its original Zoroastrian doctrine.
The only tangible work that had been left by Zarathustra was "The Gathas" through which he had expressed the gist and heart of his sublime doctrine. But what could be achieved when its language had been forgotten and thus could be no longer understood anymore?
These circumstances led the Zoroastrian priests, the *mobeds,* to learn the Gathas phonetically by heart, as sacred songs and pass them down, with astonishing precision, from one generation to the next. We are totally without the words to these priests. Without their intelligence and perseverance, the world might have lost one of the most important sources of its major philosophies and religions.

It was in the 3rd century during the Persian Sassanian period (another Zoroastrian dynasty) that a complex, sophisticated and almost perfect alphabetic system was created in order to save and preserve at least the sound and phonetics of these sacred songs.
The signs of this alphabet, like the notes of music could reproduce every single sound and accent of this forgotten language with precision and keep its original pronunciation.

This alphabet which contains 48 signs can be expanded to its more complex form of up to 53 signs; 16 vowels and 37 consonants. It is written from right to left and every word is separated by a dot.

| a | ā | ao | āo | an | aen | ae | aē | e | ē | o | ō | i | ī | u | ū |

| ka | xa | xya | xva | ga | gya | gha | ca | ja | ta | tha | da | dha |

| tta | pa | fa | ba | wa | nga | ngya | ngva | na | nya | nna | ma |

| mya | yya | ya | va | ra | sa | za | sha | zha | shya | shha | ha |

The alphabet in which the Gathas (and also the old part of the Avesta) is written. This extremely sophisticated alphabet was created in the 3rd century exclusively to preserve the sacred texts.

In order to preserve the Gathas that were still not understood, the Zoroastrian priests placed its 17 songs or chapters, each one called a " *Hat*" ,in one of the sections of the Avesta named "*Yasna*".
This section has 72 chapters among which are the 17 songs of the Gathas. They are the chapters (or hats) 28 to 34 and 43 to 51 and 53.

The Moslems Arabs' violent invasion of Persia in the 7th century, and the forced conversion of Zoroastrians to Islam lasted about 200 years and ended with the

destruction of almost all the Zoroastrian texts. Libraries, some of which were among the largest in the known world at that time, were destroyed and the totality of their books burnt. The destruction of Zoroastrian literature was to such an extent that in the 9th century only a few volumes (two or three), of the Avesta were left in Iran.
The Iranians who, following this fatal invasion, left their country and fled to India, taking these volumes with them. Once settled in India, they made extensive copies of these books. The oldest copies of the Avesta, and consequently the Gathas, that we have today, belong to the second half of the 12th century.

The Aim of Life in the Gathas

The aim of life is to live a happy and joyful existence on this earth and join with happiness the "world of thoughts" or spiritual world that is connected to the material world.
Around 70 times the words "happiness, joyful life and good life " have been repeated in the Gathas.

This happiness should not only be limited to human beings. Animals and plants also should be happy and flourish their entire lives.
One cannot lead a happy life in a miserable environment or society. The key to this happiness is to create a society based on righteousness, serenity, progress and prosperity

This sacred aim is pursued all through the Gathas, from its beginning to its end:

*" With uplifted arms O Mazda, I pray
and humbly ask for happiness.
May all my actions be attuned with Wisdom
and Good Thought, and in harmony with
the Law of Righteousness.
So that I may please You and bring
happiness to the Soul of the Earth"*

*" Thus, O Mazda Ahura
I come to You with Good Thought,
so that, I may learn through Righteousness,
the joy of both worlds,
the physical and that of the mind.
So, I may teach my companions
and lead them to happiness"*

Gathas, song 1, stanzas 1 and and 2

But, happiness and inner peace cannot be achieved unless all contribute to others' happiness, including animals and plants.

*"Ahura Mazda
has set the principles of existence
in such a way that
happiness is for the one
who makes others happy".*

Gathas, song 8, stanza 1

In order to reach this aim, one should first know the essence and the function of the two inter-related worlds: the physical and the spiritual.

The Physical and Mental Worlds in the Gathas,

Zarathustra often speaks of two different worlds, the physical or material, called *astvant* and the intellectual called *manahya* that literally means "of thought", or "mind".

These two worlds, made of material and thought, are inter-related and human beings live and move in these two worlds simultaneously. They breathe but they also think constantly.
Every organ, every cell lives thanks to the union of these two worlds. As long as body and mind are linked together and work in unison and harmony man or woman can
 live happily and lead a healthy and joyful life.
Disharmony between these two worlds, material and spiritual, creates illness and a break between them means physical death.

The physical world is ephemeral and vulnerable but the intellectual world, also called the spiritual world, is eternal. Therefore, the end of the physical body does not mean the end of life. Life continues in the spiritual world, the world of thought, which is eternal.

The laws that enable people to lead a happy life, in these two worlds, obey the principles that build the foundations of Zarathustra's doctrine in The Gathas.

Zarathustra's doctrine in the Gathas

Zarathustra named his doctrine Good Conscience *"daena vanguhi"*, and called his teachings thought-awakening words *"manthra"*. His disciples titled him The Teacher *"manthran"*, that means *"the one who teaches thought awakening songs"*.
Later his teachings were called by his disciples the "Gathas" meaning the *"Sublime Songs"*.
Zarathustra's teachings in the Gathas, are quite original. He says himself that his words *"have never been heard before"*:

*"O, seekers of knowledge,
now, I tell you words
and reveal teachings,
no one has ever heard before."*
Gathas, song 3 stanza 1

The system he built is based upon three pillars:
Good Thought, Good Word and *Good Deed*.
The pinnacle of this system is occupied by Ahura Mazda, an abstract idea and a spiritual concept: the one and only God who is ceaselessly creating, up holding and moving forward the whole system including the two aforementioned spiritual and material worlds. The term Ahura Mazda (in forms of Ahura, Mazda, Mazda Ahura and

Ahura Mazda) has been used in the Gathas around 350 times. This variety of forms seems to have been required by the metric composition of the songs.

Grammatically, this term is both masculine and feminine. Ahura (*the being, the essence*) is masculine, and Mazda (*the source of wisdom, the super wisdom*), is feminine. It is a perfect grammatical construction: a God who is both masculine and feminine, representing the strict equality of men and women which is one of the bases of the Zoroastrian system.

Zarathustra's God, Ahura Mazda, is translated by different authors as the universal source of wisdom, the super wisdom, the super intellect, the great knowledge, the great knower, the god of life and wisdom or the essence of life and wisdom.

This God was one of Zarathustra's greatest discoveries.

Hence, God was no more like previous gods a powerful, ruthless and avenging phenomenon who needed the sacrificial blood of innocent animals. Now, He / She is Wisdom endowed with all good qualities such as creativity, progress and love.

He / She is neither "omniscient" nor "omnipotent". Ahura Mazda is a progressive God, who has created a dynamic universe in which everything is in progression towards perfection.

In the English language, influenced by Judeo-Christianity, the word God is always used in the masculine with the masculine pronoun "He".

The composition He / She for God or with a neutral gender (as in Persian) may seem to an English speaking reader a little strange; moreover it makes the phrase somewhat cumbersome. Therefore it was decided to retain the more usual masculine English language concept of God and use the pronoun "He" for Ahura Mazda, in bearing in mind that Zarathustra's God is both masculine and feminine.
Ahura Mazda knows that this world has not been created perfect. There is much of suffering and pain. He hears Mother Earth who cries and complains:

"The Soul of the mother Earth
cries and complains to You:
Why did You create me?
Who fashioned me this way?
Anger, cruelty, and aggression oppress me
And none but you has the power to shield me.
Lead me to real happiness."

Gathas, song 2, stanza I

Therefore the world needs evolution and progress towards perfection "*haurvatat*". That is why Ahura Mazda created human beings as co-workers, as colleagues, as friends to help Him in his creative process for the betterment of this world, a world able to provide happiness for all living beings, humans, animals and plants.

In this system, the freedom of choice is absolute. It is another basis of the Gathas' teachings.

Every man and woman can freely choose his or her way of life and vision, good or bad. And this freedom of choice makes of every man and woman a responsible person; responsible for their own happiness or misery:

"O Mazda
While in Your thoughts,
You created at the start
body, wisdom, and conscience for us,
and invoked life in us
and enabled us with words and deeds,
You intended that we choose
our way of life and existential doctrine
as we see fit".
Gathas, song 4, stanza 11

This responsibility also gives a meaning to human existence, which is to lead a happy life, but it also indicates a direction, which is to help Ahura Mazda improve the imperfections of this world.

Those who wish to make a good choice for a happy life, in Zoroastrian terms, need to choose the wisdom that will lead them to the source of it, to Ahura Mazda.
Wisdom "*khratu*" means the power that enables people to distinguish between "good", and "bad"; righteousness and deception, justice and injustice, progress and stagnation, serenity and anxiety, love and hatred, friendship and animosity, joy and sadness, prosperity and misery.
"Good" means the forces that move people towards happiness and "bad" the forces that prevent them from reaching it.

In consequence, Wisdom is better than any knowledge. Knowledge that is not led by wisdom is destructive; on the contrary, knowledge that is led by wisdom leads to happiness. The world created by Ahura Mazda, is continuously in movement, evolution and progression towards perfection.

The creative forces called *"spenta mainyu"*, literally *progressive mind*, refresh and renew this world all the time.

Men and women, in order to achieve a happy life and create a happy world, should harmonise their thoughts, words and deeds with these creative forces, or *spenta mainyu*. They should actively take part in this creative process and help Ahura Mazda on the road of evolution.

The attributes of Ahura Mazda and how they Function

Ahura Mazda, possesses six attributes that are pure abstractions. They have no individuality and no mythology. They are spiritual ideals and play a fundamental role in the Gathas' system. Throughout the songs in the second part of this book, these attributes have been written in bold characters.

They are:

- **Righteousness** or *"Asha"*.

It is the first and highest attribute of Ahura Mazda, mentioned 162 times in the Gathas.

Zarathustra observed that a graceful and orderly movement goes on all around in nature. Everything has rhythm and every thing follows a ceaseless succession of changes. Seasons, days and nights, movements of stars, sun and earth all obey a basic law that he named *Asha* (or Arta) meaning Righteousness. It is the axis around which the ethics of Zarathustra and the entire structure of his philosophical system revolves.

The thoughts, words and deeds that are in tune with Righteousness are qualified "Good" because they help the world progress towards happiness and perfection. On the contrary, the thoughts, words and deeds that deviate from Righteousness are qualified "Bad" because they stop progress, causing stagnation and creating misery and sorrow.

Zarathustra longs to create a culture based on Righteousness.

But to be a good Zoroastrian, it is not enough to be righteous; one should also fight deception and lies with all one's power.

"Against the followers of deceit
who attempt at every moment
to prevent doers of right
from progressing in life
and development of the country,
we, with our full force and spirit shall battle
the lies in them,
Thus, I know O Mazda,
with this aim, we shall walk on the path
of Your doctrine".
                      Gathas, song 11 stanza 4

- **Good Thought** or *"vohu manah"*.
It is the second attribute of Ahura Mazda.
In the Gathas it has been repeated 127 times.
Good Thought emanates from Ahura Mazda. Its mission is to direct individual thoughts towards Righteousness. It is through Good Thought " *Vohu Manah*" that Zarathustra longs to reach Ahura Mazda. It is also through Good Thought that he tries to lead people on the path of Righteousness.
Zarathustra asks Good Thought to bestow its power on his disciples so that they can defeat deception in deceivers.

- **Self-Dominance** or *"Khashatra* " is the third attribute of Ahura Mazda. It has been mentioned in the Gathas for 64 times
Self-Dominance is the power that aims to master the negative and destructive emotions in one's inner world, letting the radiance of Ahura Mazda reaches the self. It is the best sovereignty human beings can have.

- **Serenity,** or *"Armaiti* which is Ahura Mazda's fourth attribute follows the state of Self-Dominance.
This word has been mentioned 40 times in the Gathas. It is in the state of Serenity that one can find the inner peace and the true happiness *"ushta"*.

- **Evolution and Perfection** or *"Haurvatat"* is the fifth attribute of "Ahura Mazda". It has been mentioned 11 times.
As we said previously, this world has not been created perfect. There is illness, sorrow and unsatisfied desire. There is separation from those we have loved and lost. There is ignorance, cruelty and greed. There are lies and deceptions.

Therefore, this world needs evolution towards perfection. *"**Hauvartat***" implies that nothing in this world is static; everything is in the process of moving, and becoming. And perfection means the elimination of all the deceptive forces of darkness and creating a new world based on Righteousness.

- ***Immortality*** or *"**ameretat**"* is the sixth attribute of Ahura Mazda It is used 14 times in the Gathas.
  The concept of Perfection is often used with Immortality.
  A perfect world leads to an immortal world.
  In this ideal and perfect world where there are no evil and destructive forces, immortality takes place.
  In the Zoroastrian concept, eternity does not mean "forever" but "beyond time". Life continues in the world of thoughts *"Manahya"* which has its own laws and standards.

"Now I have to speak,
of what the progressive Mazda told me,
and listening to these words is the best way
for those who hear my teachings
and appreciate them.
They shall achieve Perfection and Immortality,
and with deeds generated through
Good Thought, shall find their way to
Ahura Mazda".

Gathas, song 10 stanza 5

This immortal world that Zarathustra speaks of, is the ultimate aim. It is in this world that the Abode of Songs *"garo demana"* or the paradise of Ahura Mazda's is situated.

Those who have lived through Righteousness, and have taken the path of Ahura Mazda will reach this house and co-exist with Him for ever.

These six attributes together with wisdom that is integrated in Ahura Mazda are in Avestan language called *"Amesha Spenta" or* "immortal progressive forces".

These attributes and forces that Zarathustra continuously speaks of, are neither advice, nor even guidance; they are neither orders nor commandments. They are phenomena that Zarathustra discovered and comprehended in the depth of his thought about the existential world and the way it functions. He taught them to people who were interested in creating a specific outlook on life: an outlook able to lead them to serenity and happiness.

People are free to accept them or to reject them. Accepting them doesn't bring "salvation" in the biblical sense and rejecting them is not a "sin", because these two concepts have no meaning in the Gathas.

In contrast, the Gathas continuously insist on being in tune with Righteousness and five other Ahura Mazda's attributes and fighting deceptions and lies.

In the dynamic and ever changing of Zoroastrian system, every phenomenon, including Ahura Mazda is progressive and expanding. In this ever changing world, men and women, throughout their lives have to decide and choose between the opposite forces of good and evil. They are free to choose, and this freedom of choice is a gift they should preserve dearly. The Zoroastrians should always choose the forces that pull the world towards serenity and happiness. That is what "progress" means in Zarathustra's existential philosophy.

The Assembly of Magi

More than 3700 years ago Zarathustra created the first fellowship for those who were seeking to understand the phenomenon of existence through wisdom. He called it the *"Assembly of Magi"*

In this assembly, the members, called *"magavan"*, could talk about existence, life, death, happiness, serenity, love, separation, deception, wickedness friendship based strictly on wisdom.
Zarathustra's pupil's called him *"manthran"*, the Teacher, the Master.
Magi is a plural word, which was used 2000 years later in the Bible, referring to the "three magis". This word comes from *"maga"*, a word that has been repeated eight times in the Gathas. It means great, high in wisdom, those who search through wisdom *"khratu"*.
In his Gathas, Zarathustra has devoted seven stanzas to praise, with the best words, the members of the Assembly of magi *"magavan"*:

*"O Ahura,
come to us now as we turn to You
for love and goodness,
and tell us
when will You acknowledge,
with Your keenness of perception,
the "Assembly of Magi"?*

Gathas, song 6 stanza 7

*"The reward that Zarathustra
has promised to the Assembly of Magi
is the Abode of Songs
which from the start
has been the place to reach
Ahura Mazda.
I give you this good news
which is achieved through
Good Thought and Righteousness."*

Gathas, song 16, stanza 15

Three thousand years later, one of the greatest Persian poets, Hafez, of 14th century, praised as much as he could and with infinite veneration "the Master of the Assembly of Magi" or "pir e moghan", referring to Zarathustra throughout his "Divan".

He heard the message of freedom from the "the Master of the Magi", and found the light of God in his tavern of wine:

*"If in the Assembly of Magi, they cherish me
it is because the fire that never dies, burns in my heart"*

*"The Master of Magi recites the words of wisdom
But you o fanatic, I regret, I don't believe you "*

*"As long as the taverns and wine exist
I shall sing the praises of the Master of Magi"*

Hafez (14th century)

The Way Zarathustra was teaching

A short look through the songs of the Gathas clearly shows Zarathustra's way of teaching.

His approach is astonishingly modern. One can say timeless. It is based on stimulating the thought, awakening the brain, widening and refreshing one's outlook on life.

The method he uses is based on *"asking questions and searching for the answers"*.

He doesn't accept anything unless he understands it with his own wisdom *"khratu"*.

He asks questions about everything, from apparently the least important events in life to the greatest phenomena in the existential world. He asks over and over again and never rests until he receives the answer. He knows that nothing should remain in the dark. It is in the darkness that doors open wide to deception and superstition.

Zarathustra asks more than 100 questions. Song 9, is composed exclusively of questions.

But whom is he asking, and from whom is he expecting to receive the answers?

His method is to go deep into his thoughts, to their furthermost reaches. It is in the deepest place of his thought that he connects with the "source of wisdom" and meets Ahura Mazda face to face.

" O Mazda Ahura,
The moment I knew You in my thoughts
I realized that You are the start
and the end of existence..."
Gatha, song 4 stanza 8

He then continues questioning. He wants to know every thing: *What is life? Where is its direction? What is its sense and meaning? How can a happy life be set up ? How are the events in life shaped and where are their sources?*

He asks all these questions to Ahura Mazda. He wants to know again, who has created the earth, sun, moon and stars? Who has created Righteousness and Good Thought? He asks:

"O Ahura Mazda,
for whom did You create this joyful
and prosperous world"?

He asks again:

"O Ahura Mazda,
where is the source of a happy life
and what is the reward of the one
who looks for such a life"?

Tell me, tell me O, Ahura Mazda.
It is with questions and answers that Zarathustra builds his outlook on the existential world and arrives at his teachings.
That is why there is not a single contradiction in the Gathas and nothing remains in darkness or confusion. Everything is as limpid as water from a spring and as bright as a sunny day.

The three basic prayers in Zarathustra's doctrine

Even though there are many joyful festivities in Zoroastrianism that are all a kind of prayer. There are three basic prayers that can be recited at any time or anywhere: in front of a beautiful sunrise or sunset, in a beautiful meadow full of flowers, in front of a blazing fire, on different occasions such as marriage, anniversary initiation to Zoroastrianism, a victory in life and so on.

There are no rules on how they should be carried out.
These prayers can be recited, according to the mood of the person, in a loud or gentle voice, with or without rhythm, with or without music ... and so on.

They praise righteousness, freedom of choice and justice.
Even one of them (Yatha Ahu) indicates clearly that not only should a political leader be elected but also that one's own god, can be chosen.

1- Ashem Vohu
"prayer to Righteousness"

The path is the one and that is Righteousness,
Righteousness is happiness
And happiness belongs to the one
who wants Righteousness
only for the sake of Righteousness.

Yata Ahu
"The principles of Choice"

As the creator of existence (Ahura Mazda),
who has created the world on the basis of
Righteousness, should be chosen and praised,

In the same way, a leader, who through
Righteousness, brings the world towards
happiness, should be elected and praised.

These two principles of choice have been granted by
Good Thought, so that the actions in life be made in
the name of Ahura Mazda and the people.

Yengeh Hatam
"Homage"

We admire women and men
whose thoughts and actions
are alien to lies and deceit.
Because Ahura Mazda
knows the everyone's thoughts
and inner world, and judges all
with measure and justice.

Zarathustra and his family

In the Gathas, the name of Zarathustra or Zoroaster (as he is called by the Greeks) is Zarathushtra. His name has been mentioned 16 times. It means *"Bright Golden Star"*. According to Zoroastrian traditions, he was born on the 27th of March 3773 years ago or in 1767 BC.[1], in the land of the Aryans *"aiyrana vaejah"*, situated today somewhere between the North East of Iran, the West of Afghanistan and the South of Tajikistan.

Pliny the Roman scientist and historian of the first century, wrote *"Zarathustra was born with a smile on his lips"*, and the Avesta writes that *"Zarathustra was born with a smile lived with a smile and died with a smile.*

His father was named Pourushaspa of the family of Spitama and his mother was called Doghdova. Zarathustra was married to Havovi (meaning self-going).

1- *Apart from this date accepted by all the Zoroastrians in the world , there are many other dates, often fantastic, imaginary or even" political", given by different authors throughout history. These dates vary between two extremes of 8500 years ago (Aristotle) and 7th century BC (some contemporary authors) !*
However, the linguistic structure of the Gathas shows that it is older than Sanskrit, the language of the Rig Veda, which is dated around 1500BC. It is very probable that the date of 1700 BC is correct since it is confirmed by most scholars, including mary Boyce, (Oxford University) and Zabih Behrouz, the great Persian scholar who undertook a thorough study on the subject.

They had six children: Son,"Isat Vastar" *(strong settler)*, daughter, "Freni" (*loving*), son "Thriti" (third*)*, son "Urvatatnara" (*befriending people*), daughter,"Hvare chitra" (*sunny face*), and daughter, "Pouruchista" (*full intellect*).

At the age of 30, after passing years of meditation, observation and thinking in the high mountains of the East of Iran Zarathustra discovered the greatest principle on which he based his timeless existential philosophy:

"The aim of existence is to lead a happy life and the aim of life is to take part in the betterment of the world, where every living being, humans, animals and plants live in peace and plenty".

He revealed this principle and the way to attain it through his songs the Gathas that you will read in the second part of this book.

Zarathustra died at the age of 77 and his soul "*urvan*" and conscience "*daena*" passed forever into the House of Songs, " *Garo Demana*", the paradise of Ahura Mazda.

His grave has not yet been discovered.

Zarathustra and Europe 2500 years of history

For more than 2500 years, Zarathustra has featured in the mythologies and the collective subconsciousness of not only the Persians and Central Asians, but also the Europeans. The Ancient Greek philosophers constantly used his name as a symbol of knowledge, but astonishingly, many of them protected their own philosophical or scientific work under the fictious cover of his authority.

It is an established belief that the great philosophers such as Pythagoras, Plato and many others studied at the school of Zarathustra.

This passion for Zarathustra in the West had begun in the 5th century BC. In this period the Persians, dominating world affairs, had created a vast empire made up of 28 nations including Greece, Egypt and India. East and West were unified and this was to last for over 200 years.

Thanks to Zarathustra's reform, the Persians promulgated in an unprecedented way the most tolerant and humanitarian ideas, in complete contrast to those who had preceded them.

They had learned that *"the truth does not solely belong to any people, any country, and any race"*

It was within this Zoroastrian atmosphere, which permitted the abandoning of all the religious dogmas and formalisms, which the first Declaration of Human Rights was drawn up in the 6th century BC under Cyrus the Great.

According to this chart, engraved 2541 years ago on a clay prism, and preserved today in the British Museum, all the people of the Empire could enjoy the freedom of faiths, languages, customs, owning property and choice of their place of abode: *"I have granted to all humans the liberty to worship their own gods and ordered that no one can ill-treat them for this. I ordered that no house should be destroyed. I guaranteed peace and tranquillity for all humans. I recognized the right of everyone to live in peace in the country of his choice ..."*
It was the first humanitarian and liberating revolution in history. In particular, women were granted equality with men. The French specialist of Zarathustra Paul du Breuil writes *"the Persian women enjoyed unprecedented liberty throughout the whole of Antiquity, thanks to Zarathustra's reform. Before that, women had really been slaves. For instance Aristotle considered that women had no soul"*
It was also in this context that the Jews were liberated from their Babylonian captivity by Cyrus and the Temple of Jerusalem, destroyed in the 7th century by the Babylonian Nabuchodonosor, was rebuilt by Darius. The Jewish prophets such as Isaiah, Hezekiah, Daniel, Jeremiah named Cyrus in the Bible "the Saviour"

A revolutionary vision of humanity was now established. It was based on liberty and transcendence.

The liberation of the Jewish people by Cyrus, the reconstruction of the temple of Jerusalem by Darius and the gathering of the traditions of the Torah by Artaxerxes – the three Zoroastrian kings of Persia – and the massive return of Jews from their Babylonian captivity induced a beneficial review of the ancient Jewish laws. The prophets of Israel then encompassed, with great lyricism, the Zoroastrian vision into theseew Laws

The collapse of the Persian Empire in the 3rd century B.C. in no way reduced the prestige of Zarathustra. On the contrary, during the Hellenistic period and then during the Roman period, the passion for Zarathustra took such hold that there was no better way of lending weight to a scientific or philosophical work than to attribute it to him. This passion became so intense that nearly all sciences, including alchemy and astrology began to be attributed to Zarathurstra! In 1 AD, Mithraïsm, an ancient Persian religion, which had been integrated into Zoroastrianism, became the official religion of the Roman Empire. It remained so, for about three hundred years, until the advent of Christianity. It was a religion of mystery made up of seven levels or degrees of spiritual elevation. Nowadays, thousands of temples created to the glory of Mithra, the Sun, have been discovered all over Europe.

From 4 AD, Christianity gradually replaced Mithraïsm in the Roman Empire. As the former did not have any ritual tradition of its own, it absorbed nearly all rituals and the symbolic dates of the Mithraists. In particular the 25th of December, the longest night of the year, which was

Mithra's date of birth, became that of Christ's. Sunday (day of the sun), the holiday of the Mithraists, became the holiday of the Christians. The Christmas tree, holy bread and many more customs entered, in this way, the Christian tradition. The Christian priest would furthermore be called "Father", in keeping with the title of the great master of the 7th degree of the Mithraists. Centuries later Mithraïsm became one of the basic components of freemasonry.

In the meantime biblical traditions tried repeatedly to recover and reabsorb Zarathustra into the Semitic universe. They referred to him sometimes "Abraham's initiate", and sometimes "Annunciator of Jesus". Many Zoroastrian concepts entered Christianity as well. More especially the Christian God became "the light released from darkness", as asserted by John the Apostle. In the 7th century Moslem Arabs invaded the Persian Empire, Zarathustra's homeland. This violent invasion went on for nearly two centuries during which what remained of the Zoroastrian civilization of Persia was almost wiped out. "In six months hundreds of thousands of burnt books looted from the libraries heated the water tank of the public baths" wrote the Arab historian Ibn Khaldoun.

However, in Europe Zarathustra was not dead but relegated to Paganism; the confusion and the absurdity regarding him went so far that during the whole of the Christian Middle-Ages, Zarathustra was called prince of the Magi. This when the magi by contrast were mistaken for magicians! Even the invention of the Jewish Cabala was attributed to him!

This confusion continued until the Renaissance. At this time the great and influential Byzantine philosopher of the 14th and 15th century, Giorgius Plethon, who was initiated into the Zoroastrian philosophy by his Jewish master Eliaus, tried to set up a universal religion made of Zoroastrianism and Platonism to replace the three Jewish, Christian and Islamic religions. He did not succeed. However, his ideas spread among the European elite and flourished within the Platonic academy in Florence. They became the basis of the process leading to humanism in Europe during the Renaissance.

From that period on interest in Zarathustra was reborn. However everything had to be rediscovered, including the language in which his thought had been transcribed but had been forgotten for about 2000 years.

In the 17th century research started, but the political climate of the time, passionate and marked by sectarian quarrels between Christians, Jews and humanists, did not permit any meaningful progress. It was only in the 18th century that the French scholar, Anquetil Duperron, succeeded in translating the Zoroastrian texts gathered in a collective book called "the Avesta".

But contrary to what Duperron had previously thought, Avesta was not "the work of Zarathustra". It was made up of disparate texts written at least centuries and sometimes even more than a thousand years after or before Zarathustra.

Nevertheless, the translation of Avesta provoked passionate discussions in Europe among philosophers and writers.

Voltaire, Grimme, Didérot, Goethe, Von Kleist, Byron, Worthsmith, Shelley and later Nietzsche and many others joined this ideological turmoil.

Great musicians participated as well. Rameau included Zarathustra in his opera "Zoroastre", Mozart in his "The Magic Flute" and Richard Strauss in his symphony "Thus Spake Zarathustra".

The main interest for the European intellectuals in Zarathustra was that they thought they had found a weapon against Christianity. To them the Church no longer had the monopoly of truth. Truth could also be found in a non-Christian tradition, much older than Christianity.

In reaction, the Christian intellectuals counter-attacked accusing Duperron of being a fraud and the translation of Avesta a forgery. At this point other philologists joined the battle. Three years later another translation of Avesta made by the German linguist Kleukers proved that Duperron was right and Avesta entered forever the field of scientific research.

It still took another thirty years until the last doubters gave in and recognized its authenticity. Despite this victory everything was not yet resolved. In particular the problem of the Book of Zarathustra, the Gathas, continued to be a mystery. As I mentioned previously the language of the Gathas had sunk into oblivion for about two thousand years. Throughout all this long period the Zoroastrian priests having learnt the sacred Gathas' words by heart, and without knowing either the language or its meaning, recited them in the fire temples.

In 1861 the brilliant philologist Martin Haug, by separating the Gathas of Zarathustra from the rest of the Avesta, succeeded in translating them (despite the fact that his translation included a certain number of serious errors). Further philological and historical research was able to prove that those 17 chapters of the Gathas, were the exact words that came from the mouth of Zarathustra nearly 4000 years earlier!

The gist of Zarathustra's ideas expressed in the Gathas was brought to the limelight in 1883, just a few years after the rediscovery of the texts of the Gathas, by one of the greatest philosophers of our time, *Friedrich-Wilhelm Nietzsche*, in his book *"Thus Spake Zarathustra"*.
With great sensitivity and intelligence he was able to grasp and capture the essence of Zarathustra's thought, retranslating it in the form of a colourful philosophical novel. This work fundamentally changed Western thought of modern times.
Since 19th century hundreds of books and articles have been written by Western scholars and academics on the influence of Zoroastrianism either on Greco-Roman philosophies or the Judeo- Christian-religions. However on the 24 October 1976, an unprecedented occurrence took place.

In front of a selected audience of some three hundred people (made up of respected specialists in the field, including the prelate of the Catholic Church and a number of cultural and political Western personalities) one of the most important figures of the Christian world, Cardinal Franz Koenig, the archbishop of Vienna made an unforgettable speech. The title of his lecture was "The Influence of Zarathustra in the World". It was the first time that a personality of such importance in the Catholic world was analysing, with such erudition, the great influence of Zoroastrianism on Judeo- Christian religions and more broadly on the world.

The text of this speech (published in 2003 in three languages, English, French and Persian) by the "European Centre for Zoroastian Studies", shows how much the Christianity, in particular, is indebted to Zoroastrianism.

Quick reference to the key words in the Gathas and their meanings in English

Ahura Mazda	Creative Essence of Wisdom and Life ; God of Life and Wisdom; Intelligent Existence
Amesh Spenta	Immortal creative forces (a non Gathic word)
Ameretat	Immortality
Armaiti	Serenity
Asha (or Arta)	Righteousness
Asho(or Ashavan)	Righteous
Astvant	Physical and material world
Chinvat	Sorting Bridge
Daena	Conscience
Daena Vanghui	Good Conscience(the name of Zarathustra's doctrine)
Dregvant	Deceiver
Druj	Deception, Lie
Gaetha	Living world
Garo Demana	Abode of Songs
Gaya	Life
Geush Urvan	Soul of the World
Haurvatat	Evolution and Perfection
Khashatra	Self-Dominance
Maga	Great, Seeker of Wisdom
Magi	Plural of Maga
Mainyu	Mind, way of thinking

Manahya	Spiritual or mental world
Mazda	Universal Wisdom
Manthra	Thought provoking words
Manthran	Teacher of the manthra
Saoshyant	Benefactor, Saviour, Liberator
Seraosha	Inner-Voice, Inspiration
Spenta	Progressive and Progressing
Spenta Maiyu	Progressive and progressing mind
Ustha	Happiness; Shining happiness
Vohu Mana	Good Thought, Good Mind
Yasna	Veneration.

Names in the Gathas

Bendav An enemy of Zarathustra

Ferashaoshtra Hvogva A disciple of Zarathustra

Jamaspa Hvogva-A disciple of Zarathustra, Brother of Ferashaoshtra and the husband of Pourchista, Zarathustra's daughter

Maidhyoi-Maha Spitama A cousin of Zarathustra

Pourchista The youngest daughter of Zarathustra

Vishtaspa The king of Bactrian who joined Zarathustra

Yama (Jamshid) Vivangan The legendry first king of the Aryans who migrated from the Siberian steppes to the Iranian high lands.

*O, seekers of knowledge,
now I tell you words
and reveal teachings,
no one has ever said before.*
    Song 4, stanza 1

The Gathas
The Sublime
Songs of Zarathustra

Song 1 (Hat 28)

Zarathustra's prayer for happiness and power to make the Earth a happy planet

1-With uplifted arms, O **Mazda** I pray
and humbly ask for happiness.
May all my actions be attuned with
Wisdom and **Good Thought**
and in harmony with
the Law of **Righteousness**
That I may please you and bring
happiness to the Soul of the Earth

2-Thus, O **Mazda Ahura**
I come to You with **Good Thought**
so that, I may learn through **Righteousness,**
the joy of both worlds,
the physical and that of the mind.
In this way, I may lead my companions
to happiness.

3-O **Righteousness, O Good Thought,**
I shall sing you songs that no one
has sung before.
Then, I shall offer them
to **Mazda Ahura,**
and to those who have attained
the power of **Self-Dominance,**
and have crossed into the realm of **Serenity.**

4- I who have attuned my soul
 to **Good Thoughts,**
know that actions
in the name of **Ahura Mazda**
have their rewards.
So, as long as I have the will
and the strength, I shall teach others
to strive for **Righteousness.**

5-O **Righteousness**
When shall I see you?
I, who have known **Good Thought**,
when shall I find the path that leads
to the most progressive **Ahura**?
And listen to the guiding voice of **Mazda**?
With this edifying force
we shall overcome deception in deceivers
and convince them to choose
the radiant side of existence.

6-O **Good Thought**
Come forth and grant me a long life
on the path of **Righteousness.**
O **Mazda Ahura,**
through Your sublime words
give me (Zarathustra),
and my companions
Your powerful support
that we may triumph over
the malice of our enemies

7-O **Righteousness,**
bestow upon us the reward
which is the gift of **Good Thought.**
And you, O **Serenity,**
fulfil Vistaspa's wishes and mine.
And finally, O **Mazda**
grant us the strength to successfully spread
through this world Your sublime message.

8-Lovingly, O **Ahura,** *I pray to You*
You who are the most excellent
and in harmony with utmost **Righteousness.**
Grant to noble Ferashaoshtra,
to me, and all the wayfarers on your path
the sublime and everlasting **Good Thought.**

9-O **Ahura,** *may we not fail You*
by abusing Your gifts and trouble
Righteousness *and* **Good Thought.**
We are united in offering You our praises.
For we consider You most worthy of
invocation.

10-O **Mazda Ahura,**
fulfil the desire of those
whom You know to be in harmony with
Righteousness *and* **Good Thought.**
For I know,
words spoken from love
will never be left unanswered by You.

11- O **Mazda Ahura,**
I who have always abided
by the principles of **Righteousness**
and **Good Thought,**
show me then O **Mazda Ahura,**
how I should teach Your sublime thoughts
as they emanate from Your profundity,
and your words, as they come
from Your mouth,
so that, I may explain
how a blissful life is attained.

Song 2 (Hat 29)

Zarathustra is chosen to make the oppressed Earth a happy planet.

1- The Soul of Mother Earth
cries and complains to You:
"Why did You create me?
Who fashioned me this way?
Anger, cruelty, and aggression
oppress me.
And no one but You has the power
to shield me.
Lead me to real happiness".

2- **Ahura** asks **Righteousness:**
"Do you know a guide who can lead the
sorrowful Earth towards happiness?
And if there is one, find me that person.
That we may support and offer him or her the
power to undo deception in the deceitful and
oppression in the oppressor".

3- **Righteousness** *replied:*
"I know no one in this world totally free from injustice.
Truly, I know of no one who can support the just against the unjust.
Should I find such a person, I would hurry to his or her call".

4- ***Mazda Ahura,*** *knows best*
what the disciples of the false gods
have done in the past and
shall do in the future.
As, ***Ahura Mazda*** *alone is our judge,*
may His wishes be ours.

5- *Thus, we both,*
the Soul of the living Earth and I,
pray ***Ahura Mazda***
with outstretched hands,
and beseech ***Mazda*** *:*
"Will there be any future for
the righteous one who lives
among the deceitful?"

6-*Whereupon,*
Ahura Mazda, *the Intelligent Existence, questions me*
"Are you aware of any leader or teacher whose actions are in harmony with **Righteousness** *and* **Wisdom**"?
"Is that not why the Creator fashioned you?
And is that not your mission to guide the living world towards happiness and well being"?

7-**Ahura Mazda**, *along with* **Righteousness**, *carries an inspiring message for the well being and progress of the Earth, and to protect those who seek His protection.*
Ahura Mazda, *the Intelligent Existence then asks* **Good Thought:** *"Do you know of any person who can help the Earth"?*

8-"Yes I do".
"There is only one person
who has listened to our teachings.
And he is **Zarathustra Spitama**.
Fortified by **Righteousness**, he is ready to
take forth your sublime message through his
songs.
So, O **Mazda,**
grant him the sweetness of speech".

9-The Soul of Mother Earth
weeps again and laments:
"Am I then to accept a powerless man
with a weak voice as my protector?
I need a truly powerful leader.
When shall such a person arise,
and when will he bestow on me
his care and help"?

*10- I, Mother Earth,
implore You, O **Ahura**,
grant him, through **Righteousness**
and **Good Thought**, the power and
strength with which he may lead me
towards **Serenity** and prosperity.
Thus, I will recognize him, O **Mazda**,
as Your foremost reflection.*

*11- Where are you all?
O **Righteousness**, O **Good Thought**,
O **Self-Dominance**
when will you come to me?.
And You, O **Mazda**,
when will You acknowledge,
with Your discernment,
the **Assembly of Magi**?
O **Ahura**, come to us now as
we turn to You for love and goodness*

Song 3 (Hat 30)
Good and Evil and Freedom of Choice

1-Listen now, as I speak to you;
to those of you who have come
to seek wisdom, and those
who have already found it.
Hear then of the two basic principles.
But first, let us pay tribute
to **Ahura** and **Good Thought**,
and revere **Righteousness,**
so that you may see the light,
and attain, with the right choice,
contentment and bliss.

2-Thus,
before you are led through
the "Great Event of Choice",
hear only the best with your ears
and see with the eyes of your wisdom.
Then each of you, man and woman,
with discernment, choose one of the two paths
that are the two basic ways of thinking..

3-Of these "two basic minds",
that in the beginning,
had been conceived as twins,
and born in thoughts,
one represents Good and the other Evil.
Between these two, the wise choose Good and
the ignorant Evil.

4-And when at the first,
these two opposing minds came together,
they created "life" and "no-life".
Thus, until the end of time,
the poorest existence shall be for
the wicked, and the richest for
the righteous.

5- *Of these two opposing minds,*
followers of lies choose the worst actions,
and the disciples of the most progressive
thought, as unshakable as rock,
choose **Righteousness.**
Thus, they please **Ahura Mazda**

6-*The disciples of false gods chose*
the wrong way of thinking,
because at the moment of choice,
deception came to them,
bringing confusion and altering their
judgment.
Thus, they chose the most evil essence,
hastening into anger, and afflicting
the world and human existence.

7-But the person
who chooses the right path,
Righteousness and **Good Thought**,
coupled with the physical force produced by
Self-Dominance, come to him and bring
unshakable **Serenity** to his soul.
Such a person is Your disciple,
because he has come victorious
out of the burning test of choice.

8-And when the wrong doers
are punished by their deeds,
then, O **Mazda,**
Your light shall shine upon them through
Good Thought.
They shall learn how to flee from deceit and
embrace **Righteousness**

9-May we be among those who
make this world new and fresh!
And You, O bringer of **wisdom** and **justice,**
You, who give us the gift of happiness
through **Righteousness,** come to us,
that we may seek our convictions
in the light of wisdom and knowledge.

10- The light of such wisdom and knowledge
will empower us to shatter the power of deception,
and with our efforts and good repute ,
we shall be united, in the glorious abode of
Good Thought and **Righteousness,**
with **Mazda.**

11- *The moment you understand the function of these two basic principles, Good and Evil, that have been fixed through the will of **Mazda**, you will see that eternal happiness is for the righteous and enduring pain for the wicked.*

Song 4 (Hat 31)
Freedom of choice

1- O, seekers of knowledge,
now, I tell you words and reveal teachings,
no one has ever said before.
These words, undoubtedly, for the teachers of
lies and destroyers of the righteous world are
distasteful,
but for the wayfarers on **Mazda**'s path are
the sweetest.

2.-Whereas the teaching of lies
has blinded the mind's eye
and has robbed them of the best way,
I, like a teacher elected by **Mazda,**
come to you to teach the righteous
and the unrighteous alike,
and tell how one can live in harmony
with **Righteousness.**

3.-O **Mazda**,
What shall be that radiant happiness which
You have promised, through **Righteousness,**
to both groups?,
And what is the doctrine you have conceived
for the learned?
Reveal them, with your own words,
to the followers of Your path,
so that I can call upon men and women
towards that goal.

4-.O **Mazda, O Righteousness**
and **O Serenity,**
we who are the followers of your path,
with your justice and gifts, enable us
with the power of **Self-Dominance,**
so that with the spread of Your doctrine
we shall overcome lies and deceit.

5-O **Ahura Mazda,**
tell me
which is the better way so that I can,
in the radiance of **Righteousness**
and **Good Thought,** select the best one and
reach the highest level of wisdom and
happiness,
and on this path, with a profound vision
understand the mysteries of the events that
happen in life.

6.-The utmost happiness
belongs to the one who teaches
the secrets of a happy life to others
so that men and women can find the way to
Perfection and **Immortality.**
Ahura Mazda in tune with
Good Thoughts will increase the ability of
such a person.

*7- He is the one who at the beginning with His thoughts created happiness and **Serenity** from non-existence, and with His **wisdom** founded the world on the basis of **Righteousness** to preserve **Good Thought**. O **Ahura** with your infinite wisdom empower our limited faculty of thinking and creating so that our way will be enlightened and our lives rejuvenated.*

*8- O **Mazda**,
the moment I recognized You in my thoughts,
I realized that you are the beginning and the end of existence,
and You are the source of **Good Thought**.
And as I envisioned you with my inner sight, I knew that You are the true creator of **Righteousness**.*

9- **O Ahura Mazda**
I know that
Happiness and **Serenity** come from You,
the creative **wisdom** comes from You.
You bestowed upon men and women freedom
of choice, so they could choose their righteous
teacher and reject the corrupt leader.

10- Between the two false and true leaders
it is only the righteous one who strive to do
right deed and spread **Good Thought.**
Thus, O **Mazda,** a deceitful and destructive
leader pretending to be righteous and just can
never be Your messenger.

*11- O **Mazda**,*
while in Your thoughts,
You created at the beginning,
***body**, **wisdom**, and **conscience** for us,*
*and invoked **life** in us and enabled us with*
***words** and **deeds**, You intended that we*
choose our faith and doctrine as we see fit.

*12- And at this great moment of choice when men and women, righteous or deceitful, wise or unwise, search within themselves, to contemplate and put into words what they know, you **O Serenity**,*
enlighten us with your energy so that we overcome our doubt and choose
our path and doctrine

13- **O Mazda,**
it is only you who with your endless **wisdom**
preserve, observe, and compare all things
through the process of creation;
and that it is you who knows why,
at times, an insignificant error may deserves
a heavy punishment.

14- **O Ahura Mazda**
tell me, what kind of reward, at present or in
the future, do you bestow upon the followers
of **Righteousness** , and what sort of
punishment for the deceitful?

15- Tell me again, **O Ahura**
what is the punishment for those who
empower the deceitful and what is the
punishment who cause injury to followers of
Righteousness and detach them thereof?

*16- O **Mazda Ahura**,*
tell me,
man or woman who with knowledge and
***Good Thought** toils hard for the*
advancement and prosperity of the home, city,
and country and spreads
*the culture of **Righteousness**, how and*
when can he or she reach to You?

17- Between the righteous and the deceitful,
which one has chosen the right path?
It is truly the righteous radiant mind who
teaches people so that the deceitful could not
mislead them.
*Thus, O **Ahura Mazda**,*
*reveal to us **Good Thought**.*

18-Therefore, never listen to the deceiver
because, undoubtedly, the deceiver damages
the home, the city, and the country
Thus, withstand and battle with the
misleaders.

*19- O **Mazda**,*
may the people listen to
the advice of the wise one who
improves their life, and is righteous in
***thought, word** and **deed**, and the one who*
*in tune with Your Radiant **Wisdom**, uses his*
judgment on the basis of justice and fairness.

20- Because the one who takes the path of the
***Righteousness** shall be housed in Your*
radiant abode , and the one who chooses
deception shall live, long ages in darkness,
blind heart, and in grief,
a consequence of his conduct and action.

*21- **Ahura Mazda***
*bestows the power of **Righteousness** and*
*the help of **Good Thought**, and finally*
***Perfection** and **Immortality** on those who*
in thought and deed follow His path.

22- And this doctrine is presented to the one who promotes **Righteousness** in his **thoughts, words, and deeds** and provides support.
O **Ahura Mazda,**
such a person, for You, is the most capable friend and a guide to people.

Song 5 (Hat 32)

Deceitful Teacher And False Teachings

1. O **Ahura Mazda,**
to achieve a happy life,
families, relatives, and people
pay You homage ,
and the deceitful wrong doers,
sooner or later, shall also take Your path.
May it be that we, O **Ahura Mazda,**
in taking Your message to ill wishers,
cause their animosity to cease towards
Your wayfarers.

2. **Ahura Mazda**,
through **Good Thought** advises the wayfarers:
"we appreciate the progressive **Serenity** that is born out of **Self- Dominance** and is in tune with radiant **Righteousness.**
Thus we choose it for you, since it will be a powerful helping friend".

3- But, you,
O deceitful evil minded people
and those who cherish you due to their
ignorance, all are composed
of a wicked and devalued nature,
and your destructive acts have defamed you
in seven countries.

4.-Because you have confused the people's
thoughts to such an extent that they have
turned their backs on **Wisdom** and **Good
Thoughts**, and have stayed away from
Righteousness and fairness,
yielding their lives to corruption.

5.-Therefore,
you with your lies and ruses and deceitful
promises to those who have accepted the
dominance of lies cheat the people and deny
them prosperity and immortality.

6- *Perhaps a person with evil thoughts can obtain prosperity and fame by his actions, but You* **O Ahura Mazda,** *who remember every thing, know well through* **Good Thought** *and in the light of Your rule that, at last, the course of* **Righteousness** *and* **Justice** *shall succeed.*

7- *As prosperity cannot be achieved with the application of force, similarly the torturing of people by sizzling metal cannot be called a victory.*
O Ahura Mazda
You are more aware of the outcome of this trial.

8- *Amongst those who have been charged with evil doing was Jamshid Vivanghan whom it is reported he used cannibalism to impress people, and was recalled to trial.*
O **Mazda,** *I am only accepting your judgement.*

9- *The bad teacher inverts the righteous message and with his words confuses* **Wisdom** *and* **Good Thought**, *destroying the way of good living.*
Thus, O **Mazda** *and O* **Righteousness**, *I, with the words that come from my heart say that I shall stand against these sorts of teachings.*

10- *Because these kinds of teachers, by inverting the righteous words, darken radiant thoughts and lead people to confusion.*
They consider the worst sin is to watch the earth and the sun, with open eyes.
They destroy prosperous lands and by supporting the liars fight against the doers of right.

*11.-Such evil-minded teachers,
who are destroyers of life,
with self-grandiosity and pretension to good
deeds, steal the people's property.
They are the ones who keep the doers of right
away from the highest thoughts.*

*12- These persons who banish community
with their lies from the best deeds,
and waste other's lives with their deceitful
words by choosing the corrupt religious
leaders and troublesome politicians, are those
who by manipulating the power of deception,
strive to impede the progress of*
Righteousness.

*13- Thus,
the follower of deceit who positions himself at the lowest level of thought, longs for powers that are destructive.
But, ultimately, his deeds shall cause him to succumb and leading him to a wasted life. That is when, O **Ahura Mazda**, he with weeping and crying requests Your message, the message that makes **Righteousness** victorious over deceit.*

*14- The group of enemies, with the help of evil-minded leaders, have devoted their power and mind to prevent the spread of your message.
Assisted by intoxicating drink, Haoma, they solicit the help of wrong doers to drag the world to destruction.*

15- *As such, the deceitful religious leaders and arrogant politicians,*
who never were desirous of wanting free and enjoyable living for the people shall be defeated by the same people that eventually will find, in the light of **Good Thought;** *their path to* **Perfection** *and* **Immortality.**

16- *Truly,*
the righteous and wise teaching of the informed teacher is the best gift.
O **Ahura Mazda,**
You can free me from the hostility of my enemies, the same way that I try to relieve the followers on Your path from the hostility of the disciples of deceit.

Song 6 (Hat 33)
O Ahura Mazda, reveal yourself to me

1- A leader must judge, on the basis of **Righteousness** which is the basic principal of existence, those, whether deceitful or the righteous, or those who have intertwined good and bad deeds within themselves, with the most accurate appraisal.

2- And anyone who with **thoughts, words, and deeds**, opposes the corrupt person, teaching him and his followers the good path shall satisfy the will of **Mazda**.

*3- O **Ahura***
The one who has the best relationship
with the righteous, be it kin, co-worker,
or companion , and one who strives to inspire
the world, will be placed in the abode of
***Righteousness** and **Good Thought**.*

*4-Therefore, O **Mazda**,*
being your eternal admirer,
I shall keep away from You
ill thoughts and bad conduct.
Along this path, I shall cleanse
my kin of wrong principles,
co-workers of bad heart and envy, town
dwellers of degradation,
and all humanity of animosity and lies.

5- Thus,
in order to achieve the ultimate goal of a long life, in harmony with **Good Thought**, I shall call upon my **Inner Voice**, the "Seraosha" which is the best of all voices, for support, and I will firmly step on the solid path of **Righteousness** , to reach Your abode of commandment **O Ahura Mazda.**
.

6- Because,
I am that steadfast worshipper bound to **Righteousness,** with the best thoughts and endless love for You.
I shall endeavour in the way You wish it, to guide and improve the condition of human beings.
O Ahura Mazda,
I would like to see in You my confidant and interlocutor.

7- O **Mazda,** the sublime,
come towards me and let me see You.
So that in the radiance of **Righteousness**
and **Good Thought**,
outside of the **Assembly of Magi** I may
deliver my words to the ears of others.
Thus reveal to us our duty and the tribute we
must pay You,

8- O **Ahura Mazda**,
tell me the desired goal which I must achieve
so that I may reach it, and in the radiance of
Good Thought, pay homage to You
and walk on the path of **Righteousness,**
with perseverance.
O **Mazda**,
grant me **perfection** and **immortality.**

9- **O Mazda**,
I know that through **Good Thought**,
with the spiritual strength of **Wisdom**,
and Your enlightenment,
we shall attain the two progressive states of
perfection and **immortality**, and moving
forward in their boundless energy.

10- You are the source
of all the goodness of life,
all its happiness and all its prosperities,
those that were, are, and will be.
Thus, with Your endless love,
in the light of **Good Thought** and
Righteousness,
and the power of **Self-Dominance** bestow
them upon us so we may reap their benefits.

11- **Ahura Mazda,**
You who are the most powerful,
and you O **Serenity**,
O progressive **Righteousness**,
O **Good Thought**
and O power of **Self-Dominance**,
pay heed to my words.
And when the time of reward has come,
fulfil me with Your love.

12- **O Mazda,**
reveal yourself to me, and through
the power of **Righteousness**
give me the self confidence.
May I attain the most progressive **Wisdom**
in the radiance of **Good Thought,** and
advance with the power of **Self-Dominance**
and reach the state of **Serenity.**
May a joyful life be my reward.

13- **O Ahura,**
who watches over all things.
Help me with Your infinite love which comes
from **Good Thought,**
so that
happiness and good fortune come to me.
And you **O Serenity**, in the radiance of
Righteousness, enlighten my inner world.

14- Now **Zarathustra,** presents
his body and soul, and the core of his vision
which has arisen from
Good Thought, to **Mazda,**
and offers his thoughts, words and deeds,
and all his mental energy
to **Righteousness.**

Song 7 (Hat 34)

Where the light of Ahura Mazda shines, Wisdom shall also appear

1- **O Ahura Mazda,**
The thoughts, words, and deeds that shine with **Righteousness**, and lead the people to **Evolution, Perfection** and eventually **Immortality,**
I offer them, from inception and for You, to all men and women.

2- The one who thinks and acts only according to your teachings, will always walk with progressive **Righteousness**.
O **Mazda**, with my praise bring me closer to You.

*3- O **Ahura Mazda**,*
that which is worthy of You,
*and that which is **Righteousness**,*
I offer to you with praises.
May all men and women,
*In the radiance of **Good Thought**,*
*and empowered by **Self-Dominance**,*
*attain **Perfection**.*
***O Mazda**,*
Your spiritual power reaches those who
*choose to benefit from the **Wisdom** You have*
bestowed upon them.

4- Thus,
*in the radiance of **Righteousness***
we seek Your powerful light,
the one that eternally guides
Your followers.
With force and profound insight,
it keeps us away from harm, abuse and the
injury of falsehood.

5-O Mazda,
*When will the day arise,
and When I, along with **Righteousness** and
Good Thought, assist and help Your
wayfarers ?
And, when will my endeavours and
dedication allow me to join You ?
I, who consider You greater than all,
avoid the false gods, and the people they have
misled.*

6- O Mazda, O Righteousness and
O Good Thought,
*if I have really understood You as You are,
then guide me through life's joys and sorrows,
so that I may come to You
filled with prayer and praise.*

7- O **Mazda**,
Where are they?
Those who are Your steadfast lovers,
those who with **Good Thought** know the
value of Your sublime doctrine,
and use it, be it in happiness or suffering.
O Ahura Mazda,
You are my only acquaintance,
be then, in the radiance of **Righteousness,**
my companion and friend

•

8-O **Mazda,**
the deceitful hurt us with their evil, but they
know they may also be hurt.
They have nothing for people other than
destruction and waste.
That is why they flee **Good Thought**
and reject Your doctrine with hostility.

9-O **Mazda,**
those who with evil deeds
avoid **Good Thought,**
lose the power that is generated by **Serenity.**
They are as far from **Righteousness,**
as the misguided people are from us.

10- The Wise person says,
act on the basis of **Good Thought,**
and follow the path of **Righteousness,**
that is the foundation of **Serenity.**
And know that
where the light of **Ahura Mazda** shines,
Wisdom shall also appear.

*11- O **Mazda**,*
*The two shining attributes, **Perfection** and*
***Immortality** You have bestowed upon the*
people, shall lead Your followers to the light.
*And on this path, **Good Thought**,*
***Righteousness** and **Serenity** will offer*
*stability and firmness, and the energy of **Self-***
***Dominance** will empower them.*
With these forces emanating from You,
we shall overcome our enemies.

*12- **O Mazda**,*
What is Your desire?
And what is the praise and appreciation you
deserve?
Enlighten us, so we may comprehend
the reward of following Your message,.
*and in the radiance of **Righteousness**,*
we shall learn self-knowledge and righteous
thinking.

13- **O Ahura Mazda,**
the path You revealed to me,
is the one of **Good Thought** *and the*
teachings of **Soshiants***, the benefactors and*
liberators.
They are rooted in the principle
that "each deed based on goodness,
in the radiance of **Righteousness,**
will lead to happiness".
This then is Your reward
to the seekers of wisdom.

14- O **Ahura,**
undoubtedly, only those who in this life, strive
for development, progress, and the fecundity
of the earth, with
Good Thought *and* **Wisdom,**
and in the radiance of **Righteousness,**
spread Your Good Doctrine,
shall benefit from Your reward.

15- **O Ahura Mazda,**
With the help of **Good Thought** *and* **Righteousness,**
I shall recognize You at last,
and shall learn the most beautiful words and the best deeds from You.
And on this path,
with the support of **Wisdom** *and*
in the radiance of **Righteousness,**
I shall renew and refresh my outlook towards life.

Song 8 (Hat 43)

Happiness is for the one who makes others happy

1- The mighty **Ahura Mazda**
has set the principles of existence
in such a way that
happiness is for the one
who makes others happy.
Thus, **O Righteousness,**
for the spread of this eternal doctrine,
grant me the power of body and mind,
so I can, in the radiance of **Serenity,**
set the foundation for a happy life.

2. Because,
the best life is for the one,
who turns towards radiant energy,
and sheds light on others.
Thus, **O Ahura Mazda**,
with Your infinite **Wisdom**,
and, in the radiance of **Righteousness,**
show us the knowledge arising from
Good Thought, so that our life
would be long and be filled with joy
and happiness every day.

3. So truly,
the most rewarding goodness shall belong to
the one who, in material and spiritual life,
shows others the righteous way of happiness
which leads people to the abode of **Ahura Mazda.**
Because, it is in this way of self-creation
that he, like You **O Mazda**, will become free ,
knowledgeable, and productive.

4-O **Mazda**,
I found You mighty and progressive when I realised that You with Your power are always present with us, as a friend and companion, and with your radiance which is based on **Righteousness** warm our hearts so we benefit from the strength of **Good Thought.** Therefore, I understood that You are the one who punishes the wrong doers and rewards the righteous.

5-O **Ahura Mazda**,
I found You progressive when I saw You at the inception of life, and understood that You have set consequences for each word and deed, pain for the wrong doers and joy for the righteous,
and this practice, in the radiance of your creativeness and **Wisdom,** shall remain to the end of life and existence.

6- O **Mazda**,
where Your progressive **Wisdom** takes place,
the power of **Self-Dominance** and
Serenity shall lead the world towards
Righteousness.
And **Good Thought**, shall teach humanity
the practices of **Wisdom**. which has no use
for deceit.

7-.O **Ahura Mazda**,
I found You progressive when
Good Thought came to me and questioned:
" who are You and to whom do you belong,
and in the confusion of daily life and in the
world and yourself which path have you
chosen?".

8- First I told him
"I am **Zarathushtra**", the mighty companion of righeous, and the astute enemy of deceivers,
and until the people have found way to your radiance,
I wish to be, with all my strength, Your praiser and invoker.

9- O **Ahura Mazda**,
I found You progressive when **Good Thought** came to me
and questioned :
"Who are you praising?".
"I said I praise **Righteousness**,
and as long as I have patience and have strength, I shall be searching for it".

10- Thus, O **Mazda**,
lead me towards **Righteousness** which
I am seeking and make me attuned and in
harmony with **Serenity**.
Question me about Your expectations
and test me, since it is Your inquiries and
trials that can grant me knowledge
and strength.

11. O **Mazda**,
I found you progressive and productive, when
Good Thought came to me,
and I learned from Your words
and sensed that the spread of Your doctrine
amongst humans is difficult.
But I, will do the best that I can
to accomplish this.

12- You told me then,
to teach the practice of **Righteousness**, and
not lose hope by hostility of enemies, and
attempt to hear the guiding
voice of **Sraosha** within myself,
and in its radiance learn that,
to both groups of wrong doers and righteous,
appropriate punishment and reward shall be
given.

13-.O **Mazda**,
I found you progressive and productive when
Good Thought approached upon me and
questioned:
"What are your wishes?",
I responded: I wish a long life, so that I can
resist the deceivers and become victorious
over them.

14-. **O Mazda**,
the same way that
a friend makes his friend happy,
You too, with Your effective **Wisdom**
and, in the radiance of **Righteousness**,
grant happiness upon my followers.
It is with such a potent benevolence,
that I can rise to my feet to support those who
spread Your thought- inspiring words.

15- O **Ahura Mazda**,
I found You progressive and productive when
Good Thought came to me,
and taught that the best path to progress is
meditating in **Serenity**,
and learned never flatter the deceitful, since
they consider the righteous as enemies.

16-Thus, O **Ahura**,
Zarathushtra follows the path of Your thought, which is the most progressive and the most productive way.
In the radiance of **Righteousness**, and deeds based on **Good Thought**,
may our spiritual and material life receive strength, and **Serenity** shines within the realm of our inner self,
and rewards us with a happy conclusion.

Song 9 (Hat 44)

Respond to my questions and tell me why and how

1-Tell me, O **Ahura Mazda**,
so that I can rightly comprehend.
How shall the wayfarers on Your path
recognise You?
And when shall You teach
a friend like me ?
And again I ask You,
when shall You, in the radiance of
Righteousness, come to my aid ?
So that I may become the constant companion
and co-existent of **Good Thought**.

*2-Tell me, O **Ahura Mazda**,*
so that I may rightly comprehend.
Where is the source of the best existence?
And what is the reward for the one who seeks such a life?
And how shall the person who is elected by all,
*in the radiance of **Righteousness**,*
resolve people's difficulties and become
the guardian of progressive principles?

*3.Tell me, O **Ahura Mazda***
so that I may rightly comprehend.
*Who conceived and created **Righteousness**?*
And who put the Sun and the Stars
on their celestial path?
And taught the Moon to sometimes wax and sometimes wane?
*O **Mazda****
I yearn for greater knowledge.

4. Tell me O **Ahura Mazda**,
so that I may rightly comprehend.
Who put the Earth below and the boundless sky above it?
And who created the water and the verdant nature?
And taught the wind and the dark cloud how to flow swiftly,
and who uncovered **Good Thought?**

5. Tell me, O **Ahura Mazda**,
so that I may rightly comprehend.
Which artist created lightness and darkness?
And showed us sleeping and awakening?
And who is the one who brought morning, noon and night into existence from non-existence, in order to remind the people,
 in the radiance of **Wisdom**, *to strive?*

6- Tell me, O **Ahura Mazda**,
so that I may rightly comprehend.
Are the words I say, learn, and teach
genuinely true?
Shall **Serenity**, in the radiance of
Good Thought, spread **Righteousness**
across the world and increase the energy of
Self-dominance amongst the people?
O **Mazda**, tell me, for whom have You
created this potent and joyous world?

7- Tell me, O **Ahura Mazda**,
so that I may rightly comprehend.
Who created the energy of
Self-dominance along with **Serenity**?
And who, through **Wisdom**, established filial
love between parents and children?
With these questions,
I try, O **Mazda**, through the radiance of
Wisdom, to know You, You who are the
creator of Existence.

8- O **Ahura Mazda**,
tell me, as between friends,
I who ponder Your teachings, and question
You with **Good Thought:**
How in the radiance of **Righteousness** can I
grasp **Perfection** in life,
and benefit from a happy soul ?

9- Tell me, O **Ahura Mazda**,
so that I may rightly comprehend.
How can I enlighten my inner self with
radiant **Serenity** ?
And with the knowledge I learn through You,
how to find my way to Your abode, with the
energy of **Self-Dominance**, and attuned
with **Righteousness** and **Good Thought** ?

10. Tell me, O **Ahura Mazda**,
so that I may rightly comprehend.
Which is the best way of life?
And which is the doctrine, that in harmony
with **Righteousness,** inspires the world,
and in the radiance of **Righteousness,** lead
our lives to **Serenity?**

11- Tell me, O **Ahura Mazda**,
so that I may rightly comprehend.
How shall **Serenity** reach those who have
learned Your Doctrine?
It is to attain this goal that I recognize You as
the Highest, and I discard the false gods.

12- Tell me, O **Ahura Mazda**,
so that I may rightly comprehend.
Those with whom I used to speak,
or will speak in the future,
among these, which is righteous and which is
the deceiver ?
And who shall I turn to?
To the one who has suffered from injustice or
the one who has been unjust?
And how can I be kind towards
the deceiver who, despite Your pardons fight
against me ?

13. Tell me, O **Ahura Mazda**,
so that I may rightly comprehend.
How can I keep myself away from deceit?
And how can I stay away from those who
have chosen the path of lies,
those who have renounced **Righteousness**,
and have turned away from consulting **Good Thought** ?

14- Tell me, O **Ahura Mazda**,
so that I may rightly comprehend.
Is it possible to acquaint **Righteousness** with deceit so that the latter may be cleansed with the teaching of Your thought-inspiring message?
And would it be possible to defeat deceit in deceivers, and so cleanse the world of evil?

15- Tell me, O **Ahura Mazda**,
so that I may rightly comprehend.
You, who in the radiance of **Righteousness,** are the refuge for the righteous, when the two armies of Right and Wrong are combating each other- according to Your Doctrine- to which of these two, shall You grant victory?

*16- Tell me, O **Ahura Mazda**,
so that I may rightly comprehend.
Who is the one that in the radiance of Your
teaching shall attain victory and become the
people's refuge?
Show me that resolute leader and bestow
upon him, or any one You desire, the inner
voice of **Sraosha** and **Good Thought**.*

*17- Tell me, O **Ahura Mazda**,
so that I may rightly comprehend.
How I may under Your guidance reach my
aim – that of joining You?
And how may I instil my words and the
message, arisen from **Righteousness**, into
the hearts of people leading them to
Perfection and **Immortality**?*

18-Tell me, O **Ahura Mazda**,
so that I may rightly comprehend.
How in the radiance of **Righteousness**, my
ten sources of inner and outer strength
become potent, strong, and radiant?
Along with them, I wish to understand
Perfection and **Immortality**,
and bestow both upon the people of the world.

19- O **Ahura Mazda**,
tell me and make me aware.
When a poor person, who is truthful,
approaches a wealthy one and instead of help
receives a cold answer,
what is the punishment for such behaviour?
I am aware of the consequences
he shall receive.

20- O **Mazda,**
tell me this too.
How can the deceitful one be a- good leader?
As those who, with the help of religious
leaders and false gods, drug the world
towards injustice, pain and suffering,
or those who have never tried, in the radiance
of **Righteousness,** to improve the conditions
of life and lead the world to progress.

Song 10 (Hat45)
The two ways of thinking and living

1-*Now let me talk to you,
you, who wish to hear,
and you, who have come
from far or near,
so listen well and remember
all the words you hear,
so that the bad teachers
will not lead you to waste your life,
and the deceitful with his lies
cannot mislead you.*

2-*Now let me talk to you,*
of the two ways of thinking,
the one that makes you evolve
and the one that makes you stagnate.
The radiant and progressive thought
says to the dark and stagnating thought:
"Between the two of us,
from our very inception,
neither way of life nor wisdom,
neither belief nor discourse,
neither deeds nor conscience and soul are in
harmony".

3-*Now let me talk*
about the best way of living,
as I recognised it in my thoughts
from **Mazda,** *the source of* **Wisdom.**
Those among you who do not make good use
of this thought provoking message that I
reveal to you now, at the end,
their lives shall pass with grief and sorrow.

*4-Now let me talk
of the best way of living,
the one I discovered in the radiance of*
Righteousness, *the way* **Mazda**
has presented to people.
Mazda *who is the source of*
Good Thought *and created*
Good Thought *for work and effort.*
Mazda *who is the manifest of* **Serenity**, *and
created* **Serenity** *for good deeds,* **Mazda**
*who is aware of everything,
and cannot be deceived.*

*5- Now let me talk of what the most
progressive* **Mazda** *has told me,
a message which is best for people.
Those who hear these teachings and
appreciate them shall achieve* **Perfection**
and **Immortality**, *and with their actions
arising from* **Good Thought** *shall find their
way to* **Mazda Ahura**.

6. Now let me talk of Him,
who is the greatest and the best,
the one whom I praise in the radiance of
Righteousness, the one who adores the people.
May **Mazda Ahura**,
with his progressive and enlighting **Wisdom**
listen to our praise that we, through **Good Thought,** present to Him.
May He with His **Wisdom** teach us what is the best.

7- **Ahura Mazda**
is the creator in whom the people who were,
who are and who shall be find their success.
And you should know,
that the soul of the just, shall always be victorious and strong,
and the soul of the deceitful,
shall always live in pain.
This is the doctrine that **Mazda Ahura** has established as the basis of creation.

8. With my praises and blessings,
I face **Ahura Mazda**, and see Him through my insight and with **thought, word** and **deed,** in the radiance of **Righteousness**, I recognize him as the creator and the source of **Wisdom**, and dedicate my praises to Him and to His **House of Songs.**

9- O **Mazda Ahura**,
I praise You with **Good Thought**,
You who with Your desire, have granted the ability of happiness or pain to people,
may You O **Ahura Mazda**, in Your boundless love, also grant us the strength so that, in the radiance of **Good Thought** and **Righteousness,** we shall make the living world, people, animals and plants happy and flourishing.

10- O **Ahura Mazda**,
we praise You, in our inner **Serenity.**
You who, in the radiance of **Righteousness**
and **Good Thought**, *in your dominon,*
promise people **Perfection** *and*
Immortality,
and grant them health and strength.

11. **Mazda Ahura**,
has separated the paths of those who combat the wrong doers and that of those who oppose His doctrine.
And for the one who speaks of
Mazda Ahura *with* **Good Thought**, *and endears* **Soshiants,** *the liberators and benefactors, and the wayfarers of the doctrine, He shall be like a friend and the closest kin.*

Song 11 *(Hat 46)*

Discouragement, perseverance, and victory

*1-To which land shall I turn
and where shall I find my refuge?
My kin have abandoned me and my friends
have fled from me.
My fellow workers, too, are not happy with
me, nor are the leaders of my country, the
followers of falsehood.
Thus, O **Ahura Mazda**, in the face of such
hardship, how can I please You?*

*2-O **Mazda**,
I am aware of my weakness:
my wealth is little and my companions are
few.
Thus I come forth and face You,
look at me well, and grant me the affection
which a lover, in the radiance of
Righteousness, shows his beloved and bless
me with **Good Thought**.*

3-O **Mazda,**
When shall the dawn of happiness arrive?
The day that **Righteousness** shines in the world?
And when shall the benevolent liberators, the **Soshiants,** with their wise guidance and progressive ways shall come?
And to whom shall **Good Thought** tend ?
O **Ahura**, I, even alone, shall choose Your teaching and doctrine.

4-Against the followers of deceit, who attempt at every moment to prevent the just from achieving progress and the development of the country,
we, with our full force and spirit shall battle against them,
and thus **Mazda**, with this aim, we shall march on the path of Your doctrine.

5- O **Ahura Mazda**,
a righteous, on the basis of the doctrine of
Righteousness has a duty to warmly assist
a wrong doer who is seeking help, save him
from loss and leads him to
self-recognition.
It is also his obligation to notify other
companions so they will protect him from the
harm of evil thinkers and be his friend and
companion.

6. But, if such a righteous person does not
respond to the plea for a helping hand, he has
then himself, this time, fallen in the trap of the
deceitful enabling the deceitful be victorious.
So, on the basis of our doctrine which is our
guide, the one who leads the deceitful to
victory, is himself deceitful,
and the one who guides another to
Righteousness is himself righteous.

7- O **Mazda**,
when a wrong doer attempts to mislead me,
who else shall be my friend and companion?
Who else except my inner fire that blazes
towards You, and my thought that soars
towards You ?
O **Ahura,** it is with recognition of
the doctrine of **Righteousness** that we shall
benefit from the radiance of Your **Wisdom**
and gain strength.

8- O **Mazda,**
the deeds of a wrong doer shall not hurt those
he aims to harm.
Instead his hostile deeds shall return to him,
and he shall be devoid of a good life, and
suffer contempt.

9- Who shall, in the radiance of
Good Thought, teach me how to offer You
my best praises and the blessings You deserve?
And You,
O Master and Judge of people's deeds,
tell me:
how can I learn Your doctrine of
Righteousness and what You have said
about it?

10. O **Ahura Mazda**,
any one, be it a man or woman, who
considers good what You consider good,
grant this person the power
of **Good Thought** and
the reward of **Righteousness**.
I shall guide them towards You and
help them cross the **Sorting Bridge.**

11-*The oppressive rulers
helped by religious leaders
try to dominate the people by force
and deceit and waste their lives.
But, when they arrive at
the **Sorting Bridge**, their **conscience** and
soul shall roar at them and shamefaced, they
shall be housed in the **Abode of Deceit**.*

12-*When the children and grand children of
the wealthy Turanian elite joined*
Righteousness,
*and with inner **Serenity** and outer effort
worked for the world's progress
and prosperity,
then **Ahura Mazda**, in the radiance of **Good
Thought**, rejoined them, and revealed a
happy life to them.*

13-The one who assists **Zarathustra Spitama** to achieve his goal,
shall be recognized by all, as a man or woman of righteous principle.
Thus, **Ahura Mazda** shall grant such a person the best of life and, in the radiance of **Good Thought** and **Righteousness,** which are the bases of **Ahura's** doctrine, he or she shall benefit from **Ahura's** love.

14-O **Zarathustra,**
who is your righteous friend?
And who desires good name and progress for the **Assemly of Magi** ?
This person is truly the courageous Kavi Vishtaspa.
I shall call the people, with the words,
arisen from **Good Thought,** showing them their path to Your paradise, O **Mazda.**

15. O children of Hichtaspa Spitama,
now I shall teach you something which shall
be the best for you.
To distinguish Good from Bad there is only
one way and that is constancy
on the path of **Righteousness.**
For it is this eternal doctrine
that shall lead the people to **Ahura.**

16. O Farshushtar Hvogva,
go with your friends to the place, where the
radiance of **happiness** shines,
where **Serenity** is with **Righteousness,**
where **Good Thought** rules,
and where the greatness
of **Ahura Mazda** is apparent.

17. O wise Jamaspa Hvogva,
now with the language of poetry
and not in prose, I teach you;
thus you shall absorb it in your heart,
and praise them: whoever recognizes Good
from Evil, **Ahura Mazda** shall become his
powerful protector.

18. To the one who joins me,
I shall grant my warmest friendship,
and in the radiance of **Good Thought**
I shall promise him the best;
but, the one who confronts me,
I shall fight him also.
O **Mazda,** in the radiance of **Righteousness**,
I shall do what You want me to do,
since this is the path my wisdom and my
thought have chosen.

19. The desire of **Zarathustra**
is to build a fresh and new world.
The one who endeavours to do so unfailingly,
shall be rewarded with Immortal life, and will
achieve his aspirations in both material and
spiritual worlds.
O **Mazda,**
You have taught me all this
and made it apparent.

Song 12 (Hat 47)
Ahura Mazda, the power that creates and progress

Mazda Ahura, with His **creative and progressive power,** promotes a person to **Perfection** and then to **Immortality,** when his deeds and words are based on **Righteousness.**

2-Such a person, O **Mazda Ahura,** shall achieve the best life from Your **creative and progressive power.**
Because he is in harmony, in the radiance of **Wisdom, Righteousness,** and **Serenity,** with his words and deeds.

3-Thus, O **Mazda,** Your **creative** and **progressive power** has brought this joyous world from non existence to existence and can give it **Serenity** and stillness.

4-O Mazda,
Your **creative and progressive power**
shall stay away from deceivers,
who have refused **Good Thought**,
and shall leave them in misery
and sorrow.
But, it shall help keep the righteous
in the radiance of **Wisdom**.
Since righteous, even poor,
is precious among your people
and the wrong doer, although rich,
shall remain worthless.

5-Thus, **O Mazda,**
wrong doers shall not benefit from Your
creative and progressive power.
But, victory and happiness shall belong,
at the end, to righteous.

6-O **Mazda Ahura**,
in the blazing radiance of Your
creative and progressive power,
the destiny of the two groups,
those who are good
and those who are bad,
shall become clear.
Thus, with increasing **Righteousness**
and the spread of **Serenity**,
many seekers, at the end,
shall choose Your path .

Song 13 (Hat 48)

The best refuge is an Earth which is ruled over by Serenity

1-Righteousness shall conquer falsehood
when the deception and
lies of corrupt people are unveiled.
Then, O **Ahura Mazda**,
with increasing praise and love
the seekers of **Righteousness**
shall be turning to You.

2-O **Ahura Mazda**,
before doubt overtakes me,
make me aware of all I should know.
Shall the righteous overcome the deceiver?
And if it is so, shall the consequence
of such a victory be a happy life?

3- O **Ahura Mazda**,
You are the source of the most
enlightened teachings,
the teachings that You present,
in the radiance of **Righteousness**,
to the people.
The one who truly comprehends Your
doctrine, shall be a progressive
and inspiring person who,
in the radiance of **Wisdom** and
Good Thought, steps on your path
towards enlightenment.

4- O **Mazda,**
the one who is blessed with
Good Thought, his deeds and words shall be
inclined towards goodness and his
Conscience towards enlightenment.
And at the end with the help of **Wisdom**
that You have bestowed to him,
he shall be able to distinguish between
Good and Evil.

5- O **Serenity**,
do not allow mean and oppressive rulers to dominate us, because we desire rulers who shall lead the people, with **Wisdom, Knowledge**, and **Good Deed**.

6- In fact, the best refuge
is an Earth where **Serenity** rules .
An Earth that **Ahura Mazda,** from the beginning of creation, and in the radiance of **Righteousness**, has cultivated green and fertile, and has presented to its inhabitants the two gifts of
Good Thought and the power of
Self-Dominance.

7- You who have given your heart to **Good Thought** reject anger and resist injustice. And in this way, to spread
the doctrine of **Righteousness** join
the forces of right-minded-companions
so that you can enter the abode of
Ahura Mazda.

8- *O **Ahura Mazda**,*
how much I desire that,
*in the radiance of **Righteousness**,*
*I can benefit from the inner strength of **Self-Dominance**, and further more*
how much I desire that You reveal
Yourself to my companions and present them
*with the reward of **Good Thought**, so that*
they can become progressive
and fulfilled in life.

9- *O **Mazda**,*
how do I know that You rule, in the radiance
*of **Righteousness**, over every one, including*
those who want to harm me ?
*Thus, teach me how **Good Thought** operates,*
so that the liberators and freedom- givers, the
***Soshiants** will know that they also shall*
benefit from the reward.

10- O **Mazda**,
shall a day come when people can comprehend Your Doctrine ?
And wickedness, deceit, and greed be uprooted from the world ?
For, it is with such tools that the corrupt religious leaders mislead the people,
and oppressive and evil thinking rulers dictate with their help.

11- O **Mazda**,
when will the country be full of green and delightful pastures and the dwellings be attractive and well built ?
And when, in the radiance of **Righteousness**, shall **Serenity** cast its shade overall the country ?
And who shall resist the assault of the wicked deceitful ?
And who shall be granted knowledge, insight and **Good Thought** ?

12- **O Mazda**,
the beneficent liberators of countries,
the **Soshiants,** shall be those who,
in the radiance of **Righteousness**,
and attuned to **Good Thought**,
and Your teachings, are able to achieve the
goal that has been given to them, and shall
eradicate anger and injustice.

Song 14 (Hat 49)

Resistance against oppressive rulers

1-It has been a long time since my enemy Bandav has shown defiance against me, and has prevented me from teaching the deceived.
So You, O **Mazda**, come towards me and grant me strength, so with **Good Thought** I can save him and those like him from confusion.

2-O **Mazda**,
Bandav's dirty deeds have made me anxious, since his faith is deceit and
falseness, and devoid of **Righteousness**.
Neither is progressive **Serenity** in his heart, nor **Good Thought** is a path for him.

3- O **Mazda**,
You have established this doctrine and teaching for men and women in such a way that **Righteousness** is beneficent and deceit is harmful.
That is why I long to join with **Good Thought** and have broken with the wrong doers.

4- Those who spread anger and oppression with wrong words and deeds, and obstruct creative and right-minded people in their work, and take the side of oppression, are the corruptors that push the soul and **Conscience** of the people to malfeasance.

5- However, one who has accorded his heart, soul, and **Conscience** with **Good Thought**, and paces on the path of **Righteousness** and **Serenity**,
at last, **O Mazda**, shall be in Your **Immortal Abode**.

6.-O **Ahura Mazda**,
make me aware of what is in Your **Wisdom**
and **Thought**, so that in the radiance of
Righteousness, I can understand Your
doctrine and teach it to others.

7- O **Ahura Mazda**,
may the people, with **Good Thought** and
Righteousness, hear my message ?
If so, You shall be the witness of which kin and
companions live in tune with Your doctrine.
Thus, they become worthwhile guides for
their co-workers.

8- O **Mazda Ahura**,
I request You to grant Frashoshtra,
in the radiance of **Righteousness**,
at most happiness, and bestow such a reward
on my other companions as well.
Be we remain always the followers
of Your path.

9- *O wise Jamaspa,*
may that striving companion who is created
to liberate the people, listen to these teachings,
and that righteous person will never nourish
deceit, even in his thoughts; and those who
possess enlightened **Conscience** *shall benefit*
from the greatest rewards, and rejoin
Righteousness.

10- **O Mazda,**
in the radiance of **Good Thought,**
I entrust to You the body, soul, and life of the
righteous.
So that You remain their protector.
I praise progressive **Serenity,** *and*
I praise You who are the great might, lasting
power and immortal.

11- And I also know that the soul of oppressive rulers, and evil doers with tarnished heart, and evil thoughts shall be placed in the Abode of Deceit.

12- **O Ahura Mazda,** *Your admirers, who have made themselves attuned with* **Righteousness,** *from what kind of reward shall they benefit? And* **Zarathustra** *who, in the radiance of* **Good Thought,** *praises You with his songs, shall he also profit?*

Song 15 (Hat 50)

With thought provoking Gathas I praise You O Mazda

*1- O **Mazda Ahura**,*
who shall support my soul?
And who, except
***Righteousness** and **Good Thought** shall*
remedy my life and
my companions' difficulties?

*2- O **Mazda**,*
the one who is always hoping for
his own selfish benefits,
how can he bring freshness and joy
to the world and be effective in its
development?
*And how shall the seekers of **wisdom** who*
*live in harmony with **Righteousness**,*
bloom in the abode that radiates with Your
blazing light?

*3- O **Mazda**,*
***Righteousness** turns to the one*
who in life is guided by
***Good Thought** and **Self-Dominance**.*
It is in the radiance of these forces that he can redesign and cause this oppressed world to flourish.

*4- O **Mazda Ahura**,*
I praise You,
*and I praise **Righteousness**,*
*and **Good Thought**,*
*and the power of **Self-Dominance**,*
and I try to be the follower of Your path,
*so that in the **Abode of Song** I can listen to the words of Your wayfarers.*

*5- **O Mazda Ahura**,*
*and you, O **Righteousness**,*
*turn towards the composer of the **Gathas** and be kind to him,*
so that he with your help and support,
can guide the people towards the light.

6- O **Mazda**,
I, **Zarathustra**, friend of **Righteousness**,
with loud voice and with thought provoking
Gathas, praise You.
May You always attune my words with
Wisdom, and in the radiance of
Good Thought, reveal Your doctrine
to me.

7- O **Mazda**,
I, with the thought-provoking **Gathas**
and with the highest words praise You, and
follow Your path that leads to victory.
So that, in the radiance of **Righteousness**
and **Good Thought**, You shall be my guide
and ally.

8- O **Mazda**,
I, with thought provoking **Gathas** and with
lifted hands turn to You,
and as a free willed person, in the radiance of
Righteousness, praise You,
so that in tune with **Good Thought** I can
come closer to You

9-with thought-inspiring **Gathas**
and, in the radiance of **Righteousness**, with
deeds arising from **Good Thought**,
I come to You, O **Mazda,**
and until the day that I am not fully aware of
the deepest mystery of being,
I shall be constant and willing to understand
Your great knowledge.

10- O **Ahura Mazda**,
all I have done in the past
and shall do in the future,
has arisen and shall arise from
Good Thought,
since they are like the radiance of
the sun, and the dawn of the morning-
have been and shall be on the path of
Righteousness, and endearment of
Your doctrine.

11- O **Mazda**,
until the day I have the vital energy,
in the radiance of **Righteousness**,
I shall praise You.
May You, O creator of existence, in the
radiance of **Good Thought**,
fulfil the highest aspiration of Your followers,
which is the renovation and renewal of the
world.

Song 16 (Hat 51)

Those who are united in Good Thought, Word and Deed

1-The power of **Self-Dominance**
arising from **Righteousness**
is a precious gift which lights up
the hearts of **Mazda's** wayfarers,
and guides them to the best deeds.
O **Mazda**, grant me of this power.

2- O **Ahura Mazda**,
I offer my deeds, first to You,
then to **Righteousness**,
and thereafter to **Serenity**.
And You,
ask of me the best of what You desire,
and lead Your followers to victory.

3- **O Mazda,**
those who are united with
Good Thought, Word and **Deed,**
and come to You in order to learn,
are wayfarers on Your path.
Because You are their first
and greatest teacher.

4- **O Mazda,**
when shall Your admirers be filled with Your love?
And when shall Your reward embrace them?
How can one become the companion of
Righteousness?
And when is it possible to reach **Serenity**?
Where can we find **Good Thought**?
And when can we instil the power of
Self-dominance within ourselves?

5- **O Mazda,**
*I asked You all these questions to know:
how a person with good deeds and
humbleness, who has known creative
Wisdom and is recognized as a fair leader
by the people, can in the radiance of
Righteousness, inspire this world and
develop it?*

6- **Ahura Mazda,**
*through His sovereignty,
shall reward, to the utmost,
the one who takes steps towards
a constructive life.
But to the one who is a destroyer, and does
not strive for the prosperity of
the world, the direst consequences
be inflicted.*

7-O **Mazda**,
you who with Your progressive **Wisdom**
have created the potent Earth and life
and water and plants, grant me also
Perfection and **Immortality**, and in the
radiance of **Good Thought**, present to me
bodily health, mental power, steadiness and a
renewed life.

8-O **Mazda**,
I shall reveal Your message
to the seekers of knowledge
and shall tell them that the destiny
of a false doer is pain and the destiny of
a righteous is happiness.
Undoubtedly, happiness shall be given to the
one who delivers this thought provoking
message to the seekers.

9- O **Mazda**,
You test both groups:
the followers of **Righteousness**
and the disciples of falsehood,
through the passage of blazing fire,
and reward both groups according to their deeds.
By such action You reveal clearly this doctrine of life that is: pain for the deceiver and happiness for the righteous.

10-. O **Mazda,**
the one who endeavours to destroy
the world is a creator of falsehood and
a follower of deceit.
Thus we, my companions and I, call
Righteousness to come to us and lead
us to victory.

11-O **Mazda**,
who can be that sincere friend who will give a helping hand to **Zarathustra Spitama** ?
Who could it be except the one who is attuned with **Righteousness**, and is in step with **Serenity**?
Such a person who is the follower of **Righteousness** and **Good Thought**, rightly deserves to be a member of the **Assembly of Magi**.

12- The followers of a false leader
who have been mislead by lies,
cannot attain the happiness that
Zarathustra Spitama has promised.
Because , they seek success for their own benefit and not for the happiness of
the people.

13- By refusing the doctrine of
Righteousness and diverging from the
basic laws of existence ,
the deceiver tarnishes his **conscience.**
Thus on the **Sorting Bridge**,
he shall be reprimanded by his soul
and worry and fear shall come to him.
This is the aftermath of his words
and deeds.

14- Likewise,
the deceitful religious leaders, who have
turned their face away from justice and the
doctrine of life and nurturing,
and have misguided the people with their
deceitful teachings and dragged the world
towards destruction, shall be finally placed in
the Abode of Deceit.

15- *In contrast,*
the reward that **Zarathushtra** *has promised*
to the **Assembly of Magi**
is the **Abode of Songs** *which from*
the start has been the place to reach
Ahura Mazda.
I give you this good news that is achieved
through **Good Thought** *and*
Righteousness.

16- *Thus, Kavi Vishtaspa, in the radiance of*
the **Assembly of Magi** *and songs arising*
from **Good Thought,**
achieved the reward of inner knowledge;
the knowledge with which **Ahura Mazda**
leads us to happiness.

17- *Frashaoshtra Hvogva*
has passionately dedicated his life to the
advancement of this sacred doctrine.
May **Ahura Mazda** *assist his desire to reach*
Righteousness.

18- Jamaspa Hvogva,
in order to achieve the inner- enlightenment,
chose the doctrine of **Righteousness** and,
with **Good Thought** received that
knowledge.
O **Ahura Mazda**,
grant this knowledge to all the followers of
Your path.

19- Maidioi maha Spitama,
who devoted his life to the understanding of
Your doctrine, realised that only
with hard work and endeavour
can one learn the inner strength of this
doctrine and use it for a better life.

20.- Thus, O **Amshesha Spentas,**
you who are of one mind and one will,
you who know that we have always praised
you, teach us the doctrine of **Righteousness**
and **Good Thought,**
so that we may attain **Serenity** and, in this
way, blessing of **Ahura Mazda** and be able
to seek His help.

21- *The one who,
in the radiance of* **Good Thought,** *attained
the power of* **Self-dominance,** *and has
reached* **Serenity** *and, with his* **Word,
Thought** *and* **Deed,** *spreads
the doctrine of* **Righteousness,
Ahura Mazda,** *blesses such a person with a
clear* **Conscience.**
I, too, wish him happiness.

22- **Ahura Mazda,**
knows those who in the radiance of
Righteousness, *have come to him,
be it in the past or present.
I, too, praise them, and remember them with
good name, and bestow my greetings to them.*

Song 17 (Hat 53)
Consult your wisdom, then choose

1-Now, my highest aspirations, **Zarathustra Spitapma,** have been accomplished, since, on the basis of my **Good Thought Good Word** and **Good Deed** and their harmony with **Righteousness, Ahura Mazda** has granted me for eternity good and enhancing life.
The people, even those who feel animosity towards me have accepted His immortal and precious doctrine and adopted it in their lives.

2-*Thus, you too,*
turn towards **Mazda** *and*
open your heart and thought to Him.
Kavi Vishtaspa, supporter of **Zarathustra**
and the wise Ferashaoshtra have chosen a
doctrine, that **Ahura** *has revealed to the*
benevolent liberators, the **Soshiants**.

3-*And you,*
O Pouruchista Spitama Haechataspa,
my youngest daughter, choose as your
husband, the one who is bound to the
doctrine of **Good Thought** *and*
Righteousness.
Thus, with the name of **Mazda**,
first consult your **Wisdom** *and then*
with awareness and **Serenity**
make your choice.

4 -I, Pouruchista,
shall choose such a person
and shall love him.
Therefore, with honour among the citizens,
fellow workers, family, father and husband,
in the radiance of **Good Thought**, I shall
always be the follower of **Mazda's** path.

5-Thus, now
I, **Zarathustra**, tell you these words:
"O new brides and o new grooms,
listen to my advice with **Wisdom,**
learn and comprehend it with **Conscience**
and apply it.
Live your life always with
Good Thought, and each one of you lead the
other with **Righteousness**, so you may live a
life of happiness and fulfilment".

6- O men and women,
know that in this world deceit
is the destroyer of life, and you should avoid it
and not spread it.
Know that pleasure gained by deceiving
others is in fact the cause of pain and
suffering.
The corruptors who are at war with
Righteousness destroy happiness in their
lives.

7- And the reward of the **Assembly of Magi**
shall be yours until the day that you honour
your promises, in full,
regardless of vicissitudes of life.
But, if deceptive thought dominates you and
by breaking your promise,
you turn your back on the doctrine of the
Assembly of Magi, you shall not find any
thing except pain and sorrow in life.

8- *Sorrow and pain is for those who have been deceived and have joined the group of wrong doers.*
May destructive deceit be wiped out in the radiance of right governance.
*That men and women, may live in homes and cities, with **Serenity** and renewal, and the light of **Mazda** shall appear to them.*

9- *Distorted and corrupt thinkers who combat **Righteousness** and aim at degrading the disciples of **Wisdom**,*
work against themselves.
Where is that righteous leader who will rise against them and destroy the bad deed within them ?
*O **Mazda**, it is only under Your sublime reign that the doers of right shall benefit from the best of life.*

Main sources

Without the extraordinary works done during the past 200 years by the great linguists and specialists in comparative philosophies and religions around the world, the writing of the present book could not be possible. I am particularly indebted to the works of the following authors (*names are not arranged alphabetically*):

E.Pour-Davoud; Gatha, Bombay,1951
A.A. Jafarey; The Gathas, our guide, California 1989
A.A. Jafarey; Stot Yasn, Berlin 2001 (reprinted)
H. Vahidi; Gatha, the spiritual songs of Zatathustra, Tehran 1987
F. Azargoshasp; The Holy Songs of Zarathustra, Los Angeles 1999
A. Sasanfar; The seven songs of the Gathas, Tehran 2004
R. Shahzadi and T.R Sethna; Zarathusra's teachings, Karachi 1975
S. Inslar; The Gathas of Zarathustra, Liège, 1975
I.J.S. Taraporewalla; The divine songs of Zarathustra, Bombay 1911
J.M. Chatterjee; The songs of Athravan Zarathushtra, Calcutta 1976 (revised)
F.Bode and N. Piloo; Songs of Zarathustra
J. Duchesne –Guillemin; The hymns of Zarathushtra, Paris 1950

J. Duchesne –Guillemin; Wesrten Response to Zarathustra, Oxford 1959

K. Geldner; The sacred books of the Parsis, Stuttgart 1896

H.L. Mills; The Gathas of Zarathustra (Zoroaster),Leipzig, 1900

H.L.Mills; A dictionary of the Gathic language of the Zend-Avesta, Vol. 3 NewYork 1977

C. Bartholomae; Altiranisches Wörterbuch, Berlin 1979 (repr. 1904)

M.Haug; Essays on the sacred Language, writings and religion of the Parsis, 3rd ed., London 1884

D.J Irani; The divine songs of Zarathshtra, London 1924

Anquetil du Perron; Zend-Avesta, Ouvrage de Zoroastre, 3 vols. Paris 1771

C.de Harlez; Livre sacré du zoroastrisme, 2eme éd. 1881

J. Darmesteter; Zend-Avesta, 3 vol., Paris 1992 (rep.)

A. Millet; Trois conferences sur Avesta,Paris 1925

M.N.Dhalla; History of Zoroastrianism, Bombay 1985

E.Bahrami; Dictionary of the Avestan Words, 4 vols., Tehran 1993 (1369)

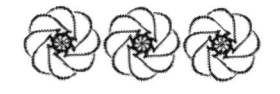

Made in the USA
San Bernardino, CA
20 June 2018